*Traveling History Up the Cattle Trails:
A Road Tripper's Guide to the Cattle
Roads of the Southwest*

Robin Cole Jett

*Other states were carved or born
But Texas grew from hide and horn*

~Berta Hart Nance~

Traveling History Up the Cattle Trails: A Road Tripper's Guide to the Cattle Roads of the Southwest
Copyright © 2011 by Robin Cole Jett
All rights reserved

ISBN: 978-0-615-41876-6

Library of Congress Control Number: 2011925346

Manufactured in the United States of America

Except as permitted under the United States Copyright Act of 1976, no part of this publication may be reproduced or distributed in any form or by any means, or stored in a data base or retrieval system, without the prior written permission of the publisher.

Red River Historian Press
109 Villa Park Drive Lewisville, TX 75077
972-353-4130

Visit Red River Historian Press at
http://www.redriverhistorian.com

Publisher's Cataloging-in-Publication

Cole-Jett, Robin.
    Traveling History Up the Cattle Trails: A Road Tripper's Guide to the Cattle Roads of the Southwest / by Robin Cole Jett
        p. cm.
    Includes index and footnotes.
    LCCN: 2011925346
    ISBN: 978-0-615-41876-6

Table of Contents

Table of Photographs 6

Acknowledgements 9

Introduction 10

Cows on a Drive 12

Chapter One: Trail Drive History 13
    Southwestern Cattle Drive Beginnings, 1850s-1867 15
    The Cattle Drive Outfits 17
    Life on the Trail 18
    Cow Towns 21
    The End of the Trails 23
    The Trails Today 25

Chapter Two: The Shawnee Trail 28
    Texas Shawnee Trail Tour 31
    Oklahoma Shawnee Trail Tour 42
    Kansas Shawnee Trail Tour 58
    Missouri Shawnee Trail Tour 60
    End of the Shawnee Trail 66

Chapter Three: The Chisholm Trail 67
    Texas Chisholm Trail Tour 1 70
    Texas Chisholm Trail Tour 2 91
    Oklahoma Chisholm Trail Tour 98
    Kansas Chisholm Trail Tour 109
    End of the Chisholm Trail 116

Chapter Four: The Great Western Trail 117
    Texas Great Western Trail Tour 120
    Oklahoma Great Western Trail Tour 135
    Kansas Great Western Trail Tour 145
    End of the Great Western Trail 151

Epilogue 152

Resources 153

Bibliography 165

Index 167

Notes 176

Table of Photographs

1. Exchange Avenue at the Fort Worth Stockyards. Courtesy Fort Worth Public Library.
2. Cattle round-up in Mexico. Courtesy Cattle Raiser's Museum.
3. Chuck wagon pulled by oxen. Courtesy Cattle Raisers Museum.
4. River crossings were dangerous business. Courtesy Cattle Raisers Museum.
5. Stag Saloon in Fort Worth. Courtesy Fort Worth Public Library.
6. Dugan wagon yard in Fort Worth. Courtesy Fort Worth Public Library.
7. Carpenter Bluff's Bridge near Dension, Texas. Photo by author.
8. Pioneer Plaza in downtown Dallas. Photo by author.
9. Dorchester's downtown has seen better days. Photo by author.
10. The cemetery is all that remains of Preston. Photo by author.
11. The Missouri-Kansas-Texas Railroad bridge between Texas and Oklahoma marks the Shawnee Trail crossing. Photo by author.
12. Fort Washita is in a state of arrested decay. Photo by author.
13. Nothing remains of Boggy Depot except the cemetery. Photo by author.
14. Ruins of coal mines sit in a farmer's field east of Pittsburg. Photo by author.
15. Inside Robber's Cave. Photo by author.
16. Fort Gibson's officer quarters. Photo by author.
17. Baxter Springs sits along the fabled US 66. Photo by author.
18. The Missouri and Kansas rivers defined Kansas City. Courtesy Kansas City Public Library.
19. The Swift packing plant at the Kansas City Stockyards. Courtesy Kansas City Public Library.
20. The Pony Express Stables now house a museum. Photo by author.
21. Monument Hill in Addington, Oklahoma. Photo by author.
22. Visit the museum inside the county jail. Photo by author.
23. The street that crosses the stream near the Round Rock marks the original cattle and pioneer road. Ancient wagon ruts are clearly visible. Photo by author.
24. Waco's suspension bridge served as a model for the Brooklyn Bridge. Photo by author.

25. Tenth Street was a busy place at the turn of the century. Courtesy Fort Worth Public Library.
26. The Stockyards of Fort Worth were anchored by the Swift and Armour packing plants. Courtesy Fort Worth Public Library.
27. Weatherford Street housed saloons and brothels. Courtesy Fort Worth Public Library.
28. The fabulous "El Castile" in Decatur greets visitors from atop a hill. Photo by author.
29. This store is the only remaining structure of downtown Spanish Fort. Photo by author.
30. The Stonewall Saloon in St. Jo harks back to frontier days. Photo by author.
31. The old store at Fleetwood sits just west of the Chisholm Trail. Photo by author.
32. African American cowboy Tom Lattimore, who took several trips up the Chisholm Trail, is buried on top of Monument Hill. Photo by author.
33. Jesse Chisholm's grave at Left Hand Spring. Photo by author.
34. Upon entering Kansas, you'll be greeted by the shadow of a trail drive. Photo by author.
35. Chisholm Trail monument on Douglas Avenue. Photo by author.
36. At Lehigh, the surveyed portion of the Chisholm Trail is plain to see. Photo by author.
37. False façade at the Chisholm Trail terminus. Photo by author.
38. Ruins of Fort Phantom Hill near Abilene, Texas. Photo by author.
39. Mission San Jose in San Antonio. Photo by author.
40. The road will take you right over the cattle trail's Llano River Crossing. Photo by author.
41. Just like England's London, Texas' version has a certain kind of charm. Photo by author.
42. The wheel along Menard's "ditch." Photo by author.
43. Bridge across the Brazos River at Fort Griffin Flat. Photo by author.
44. Thousands of cattle crossed the Red River at Doan's store. Photo by author.
45. Remnants of the past in Lone Wolf. Photo by author.

46. Old Retrop's downtown. Photo by author.
47. Frontier business in Leedey. Photo by author.
48. Fort Supply displays Kiowa ledger art. Photo of drawing by author.
49. The Cimarron River crossing is marked by a Great Western post. Photo by author.
50. The haunting landscape of the Big Basin epitomizes the beauty and isolation of the Great Plains. Photo by author.
51. The Dodge City of the 20th century teemed with culture. Photo by author.

Front and back cover: Boot on barbed wire fence near Monument Hill, Addington, Oklahoma. Photo by author.

Acknowledgements

My inspiration and passion for Western history stems from my deep admiration of many scholars. The works of Walter Prescott Webb, Patricia Nelson Limerick, Dan Flores, Wayne Gard, Terry Jordan, and Angie Debo have guided me as I uncovered the varied stories of the western past.

A large thanks goes to my son, David Jett. He has traveled with me down and up all the trails and we've enjoyed every minute of those trips. Raymond, you're a very understanding man. Ray and Chris, you are two of my favorite people. Lisa, thanks for your eagle-eye. Katherine Landdeck, Martina Will de Chapparo, and John Travis, thank you for your expertise.

And last but not least, my eternal gratitude goes out to the towns and people I've encountered as I traveled these dusty trails. I believe there are no kinder, more generous people than those who live in the Central Plains and no landscape more breathtaking. I am thankful every day for living and traveling amongst such beauty.

Introduction

Since I was a little girl, I have been fascinated with the way people have transported themselves, be it on foot, rail, or by automobile. Maybe it's because I am a wanderer myself. Whether riding my bike or driving my car, I don't like to be hemmed in, and at times I've wondered if I inherited the proverbial "itchy feet" of the pioneers.

The first explorers of the West were the many native tribes who followed the seasons and, after horses were introduced, the buffalo. One can argue that the Comanches, Wichitas, Sioux, Lakotas, Dakotas, Cheyennes, Kiowas, et. al. were the original pioneers of America, not just in movement but in spirit as well. The Plains Amerindians did not believe in living stationary, sedentary lives. Tribal members were cooperative and individualistic in a way that the Europeans who came to the "New World" never quite grasped. To the Indians, the vastness of the prairie meant freedom, and to roam was to be alive.

As the Spanish, French, and English came to the American West, they heard the call of the wide plains, too. Along with other ethnicities – Scots, Irish, Germans, African Americans, Swedes – these people saw opportunity in, and all too often took advantage of, the vast distances and open landscapes of the Plains. Attempts at permanent settlement didn't occur until well into the 19th century, however, as earlier explorers christened the Plains "the Great American Desert," fit for only the buffalo. Regardless, the emigrant roads, stage coach routes, and cattle trails that these pioneers built in order to cross the Plains tell magnificent stories of a landscape that propelled people forward.

Often, these explorations took an ominous tone. The cattle trails epitomized how exploration turned quickly into exploitation: tribes were forced off their lands, small ranchers saw the free range system disappear, and the railroads, with the backing of the government, declared eminent domain. Within twenty years of the first post-Civil War cattle drive, the railroads replaced the trails, which, a hundred years later, were replaced by diesel-powered trucks.

The need for movement remained, however. Only the routes differ. When I'm driving along through the southwestern Plains, I never can get these images out of my head: on every crest, through every draw, along every tree line, I see the fiercely independent Amerindian and the equally fierce pioneer family, both eager to find a point on the horizon to set up their territories. There seems to be a need to move here, an almost primal urge to spread one's wings.

I still see that spark in modern travelers as they make their way towards their next destination. They want to be on the go – like me, they may feel as though they can breathe a little easier as they cross the western landscape. And if they can wed that liberating feeling of the open road with an understanding of the history behind it, they can weave their modern stories with the ancient tales that make the West what it is.

Cows on a Drive

Three distinct cattle trails extended from Texas to Kansas. The mere mention of their names – the Shawnee, Chisholm, and Great Western Trails - conjures up images of rugged cowpokes singing softly to the cows on the wide-open prairie while keeping watch under a brilliantly illuminated night sky.

Regardless of our current notions, driving cattle up the trails was anything but romantic. Extending from the tip of South Texas all the way to the notorious Kansas cow towns of Caldwell, Abilene, Dodge City, and Ellsworth, the trails covered a distance of over a thousand miles – traveled on swaying horse back and sometimes on foot. The food consisted of biscuits supplemented by beans, bacon, coffee, and more beans. Days could go by before the men on the trail would see another human being, let alone a washtub. And yet the idea of driving wild longhorns along a dusty trail beyond the so-called "Western Frontier" is powerful enough to keep us modern day cowpokes fascinated.

Following the cattle trails makes an excellent driving vacation for the whole family. The trails take you from the banks of the Rio Grande, Brazos, Trinity, and Red Rivers all the way to the Great Plains of Kansas. Although several feeder trails meet up with the main road across Central Texas, it is in North Texas, Oklahoma (formerly Indian Territory), and Kansas where the trails become worthy of their grandiose reputations. Today, the trails have been either plowed or paved over, but several highways parallel the routes, at times even bisecting them. You can experience the trails through detours, markers, interesting museums, and at times witness the trails for yourself along ghostly ruts in isolated fields.

This book guides the traveler on a historical journey through wide, open spaces. Along the old trails trampled down by thousands of hooves and hundreds of cowboy boots, the prairie beckons, the cow towns holler, and the noisy, dirty, and industrial stockyards call out. By following three of the southwest's primary cattle trails, the historic-minded traveler will experience the American West in a new way.

So come along the dusty trails as we explore the American West as it was meant to be seen!

Chapter One

TRAIL DRIVE HISTORY

Exchange Avenue at the Fort Worth Stockyards.
Courtesy Fort Worth Public Library.

Driving cattle to market is nothing new. The Bavarians in the Alps have been doing it for centuries, as have the Masai on the African savannah and the Nepalese in the Himalayas. Since the beginning of the American colonies, North Carolinians practiced open range cattle handling, and the Spanish colonies followed their own cattle herding traditions. Even New York City built its commerce on cattle driving. Collect Pond centered the New York animal trade before it was filled in and became the notorious Five Points neighborhood.[1]

In early Texas, the first cattle drives maneuvered east through the dense brush of the Big Thicket to Shreveport and New Orleans. In New Orleans, the herds moved upriver by boat to be sold and slaughtered in St. Louis.

What makes the southwestern cattle drives so unique is the distance the cows were driven. No cattle drive in prior history had managed to guide herds so far and be profitable. Between 1868 and 1884, over five million cattle had made the journey from Texas to Kansas, at prices that ranged from $4.50 to $18 per head.[2] Cattle driving in the post-Civil War period added another dimension to this usually localized activity: it became a corporate-controlled, high stakes business.

The long distance trails served as a way for Texans to trade and sell their cattle, which consisted of feral longhorn that numbered in the millions. Texas did not have a railroad going north, making it difficult to ship to the northern markets. To get to the large slaughter houses of Chicago, St. Louis, and Kansas City, cattle drivers trailed the animals to meet up with railroad terminals in Illinois, Missouri, or Kansas. Along the route, some outfits sold portions of their herds to local packing houses and to ranchers in Indian Territory because either railroad shipping rates became too high or a glut on the market forced the drovers to cut the herd. Sometimes, cattle drivers bypassed the rail heads altogether and instead trailed their charges all the way to the big corporate slaughter houses in Chicago and St. Louis.[3]

Along these trails that are now known as the "Shawnee," "Chisholm," and "Great Western," distinctive cultures in America collided. They became "an important meeting ground, the point where Indian America, Latin America, Anglo America, Afro-America, and Asia intersected."[4] Black, white, and Hispanic cowboys learned tricks of the trade from each other. In turn, the cowboys had to learn to negotiate with the people of Indian Territory, where members of the Five Civilized Tribes as well as the Southern Plains tribes lived.[5]

Southwestern Cattle Drive Beginnings, 1850s-1867

Cattle round-up in Mexico. Courtesy Cattle Raiser's Museum.

In the period from 1850s to the start of the Civil War, the Five Civilized Tribes of Indian Territory engaged in cattle breeding from stock that they had brought with them from their original homelands. The full-blooded members especially took to this trade, as it forestalled the burdens of the white man's primary occupation, dirt farming. The tribes did not trail their cattle, though. They relied on Texans coming up the Shawnee Trail to buy, sell, and experiment with the sturdier longhorn breed. They also taxed cattle drivers passing through their lands.

The Civil War ground all this activity to a halt. While history books focus almost exclusively on the tragedies of the white soldiers, the Civil War proved equally and often far more devastating to the peoples of Indian Territory. Two separate factions among the Indian Nations collided in the war: older, full-blooded members who insisted on honoring the previous treaties with the U.S. government, and younger members who saw the Civil War as an opportunity to break off all ties with the whites. Members with economic and social stakes in slave society – those who owned plantations, were slave traders, and/or profited from the system – joined the Confederacy. As pro-Southern sentiment increased, Union troops abandoned the various territorial forts. Indian Territory became a semi-lawless region where raids, brutal battles that literally pitted brother against brother, and mistreatment of civilians became the norm.[6]

After the war, the United States voided all prior treaties even though most members of the Indian Nations had remained loyal to the Union. The nations had to agree to the 1866 Reconstruction Treaties, which stipulated that each tribe cede land to the railroads and white settlers, adopt all freedmen as full tribal members, and make room in the territory for the Southern Plains Indians. By 1875, after years of fighting in the Red River Wars, the U.S. Army forced the remaining members of the Southern Plains tribes onto reservations in Indian Territory.

What was the end of an era for one group, however, proved to be the beginning of another. Freedmen started to populate Texas and Indian Territory in search of adventure, work, and a piece of land to call their own. Not only did the wide open spaces entice them, but many found work in the cattle drive outfits and discovered life on the trail to be liberating. The need for cowboys was so great that black men often met with fair treatment and good wages. The demand was especially large for cowboys who were daring. For the most part, African American cowboys took on more dangerous jobs, though whether it was a personal preference of liberation after living a life in slavery, a way to "prove themselves," or because they were considered to be "expendable," is still open for debate.

The cows continued to be driven along the old Shawnee Trail to Missouri and Kansas in the first few years after the Civil War. Often, the old road proved to be more hassle than it was worth. Farmers moved into the eastern parts of Texas and Kansas and resented the cattle, and bitter ex-Confederates from Missouri still prowled around the area, looking for trouble. Joseph McCoy, an entrepreneur from Illinois, surveyed portions of what become known as the Chisholm Trail in 1867 and convinced cattle drivers to utilize this new road instead. Later, as the Chisholm Trail became more and more populated by farmers, drivers steered their herds over a trail blazed by John Lytle, which is now known as the Great Western Trail.

Cowboys and ranchers established other trails as well. Charles Goodnight and Oliver Loving, for example, forged their own road through the Llano Estacado (the "Staked Plains" in the Texas panhandle), and John Chisum took his herds west from Denton County all the way to New Mexico. The southwestern cattle trails proved to be a real bonanza for Texans.

The Cattle Drive Outfits

Chuck wagon pulled by oxen. Courtesy Cattle Raisers Museum.

While the end of the Civil War in 1865 proved to be an uncertain beginning for many Americans, Texans and citizens of Indian Territory in particular had a major advantage on their road to recovery. Due to their location in the western Confederacy, the region had seen very little fighting. Their geography proved even more fortunate, as Texas held a particular wealth that other states did not: the longhorn cattle.

Whether white, black, Indian, or Mexican, all cowboys knew the real impetus of the cattle trade, which was embodied in the sturdy longhorns. When Spanish cattle breeds interbred amongst themselves, the resulting longhorns began to dominate the southwestern landscape.[7] In a time before barbed wire, when the only fence built was to keep cattle out, millions of these cattle roamed all over Texas.

Because of the demands of the trail, cowboys never trailed alone. Instead, they joined outfits. The outfits had clear hierarchies – one could say they were semi-corporations. Owners of cattle herds contracted an experienced and trusted cowhand to head the outfit as the trail boss. Often, the trail boss owned several of the cattle he was hired to trail himself. The cowboys were hired hands, though sometimes they might also own a few of the cows they were trailing.

As the cowboys came from many different backgrounds, so did their handling methods. Cowboys combined Spanish methods of herding with the southern ways that Anglo and African American cowboys employed, such as rounding up and branding.[8]

Most of the cowboy's gear was of Spanish origin – saddles, chaps, and lassos. Black cowboys sung negro spirituals to the herds, sometimes with the words altered, to calm them down. Both Tejano and Southern recipes fed the trail drivers: beans, bacon, and black coffee coupled with sourdough biscuits and tortillas.

An outfit could be as small as ten or as large as twenty men. After the boss, the next person in command was the cook – contrary to popular belief, the cook, who most likely was a former trail hand, commanded respect. Experienced hands made up the flanks of the drive. The "greener" cowboys had to ride in the rear, eating mouthfuls of dust. The most junior member, the wrangler, was in charge of the *remuda*, or surplus horses, and drove them adjacent to the cattle herd.

Life on the Trail

Life on the trail did not prove easy. Herding in excess of 10,000 head of cattle for at least two months straight can wear out even the sturdiest cowboy. Not only was theirs a 24/7 job, they had to contend with life-threatening situations as well.

The biggest threat was weather. The trails zigzagged across a region now known as "Tornado Alley," and the cowhands experienced their fair share of twisters. Though they usually trailed only in the late spring and summer, even then they could face natural hazards, such as freak blizzards and unrelenting heat.

River crossings were dangerous business. Courtesy Cattle Raisers Museum.

The sudden heavy thunderstorms on the Plains could swell creeks and rivers, making crossings extremely difficult. In fact, the most treacherous part of the entire journey was along stream beds. The Red River was notorious for its swift and changing currents, which often hid quicksand. When fording rivers, the cattle might start to mill, which meant they'd walk in circles instead of going straight. A cowboy faced injury or even death if he got caught in one of these vortexes.

A thunderstorm invariably caused a stampede – actually, practically anything could spook the cows. When the cows stampeded, the trail hands ran their horses in a large circle in the hopes of keeping the cattle from wandering too far, and allowed the frightened animals to simply tire themselves out. Cattle usually stampeded at night after being "bedded down," as the enforced stop made them even more restless. The howl of coyotes, the hoot of an owl, or simply an expected noise in the dark could cause mayhem. In one infamous incident, a cow got its hoof stuck in an empty can of tomatoes that the cook had thrown away, and the resulting stampede lasted all night.

Humanity posed its own dangers. A chronic alcoholic could spell trouble for the cowboys, so drinking was strictly prohibited on the trail. That rule was not always heeded, however. In 1873, a drunken cook beheaded four cowboys in a dispute in the forbidding Cross Timbers region around Gainesville, Texas.[9]

Trail driving was not just hard on the humans. The cattle suffered, too. The cowboys poked, prodded and branded the animals, which remained nervous throughout their journey. The drive proved especially cruel to new mothers. While the drivers would often wait until their cattle had given birth before undertaking a drive, that wasn't always possible. When a cow did calve on the trail, the outfit deserted the calf and tethered, or hobbled, the mother cow to another cow. She was then forced to continue the drive, with her baby blaring in the thickets.

Another problem on the trail proved to be the frail relationship between the Texans and the tribes in Indian Territory. Tensions between the groups over access rights, boundary disputes, or animosity between chiefs and trail bosses resulted in provoked stampedes, shootouts, and scalpings.

Like the members of the Five Civilized Tribes in eastern Indian Territory, Southern Plains tribal bands demanded steers as payment for allowing the cowboys to cross their lands. While trail bosses mostly accommodated the Five Civilized Tribes, they would often refuse the Plains Indians. This may have been because of the sheer number of men asking for payment, or because Texans did not view the Southern Plains Indians as owning the land – the reservations, Texans believed, were federal property.

When the trail boss refused to pay toll or hand over a cow, the bands might stampede the herd at night and run off with stray cattle. Often, the outfits shot at the Indians outright while refusing the demand for toll. News traveled fast to other bands, and revenge proved swift. This happened to trail driver F.M Horton, who shot to death the chief of a Cheyenne band, Running Buffalo, after the chief had asked him for some cattle. Horton was forced to seek protection at Fort Sill when enraged Cheyennes and Arapahos accosted his outfit. After two nights of war dances, chants, and threats, Horton gave over half his herd to the men, and they finally backed off.[10]

While the cowboys relished the open prairie, they also looked forward to entertainment in the many towns along the way. Along with singing, cowboys loved to dance. The dancehalls were not always the best place for a young, inexperienced cowhand to go, however. Meeting up with shady poker games and with ladies of ill repute, the cowboys often left the towns broke. In the latter years of the drives, trips to vice districts became exceedingly rare as the outfits became more professional.

Though the dangers could be severe, cowboy recollections seem to recall the freedom and adventure of the trails with fondness. For many cowboys, trailing meant broadening their horizons. Walter Giesecke from the Texas Hill Country, for example, took his herd all the way to Chicago. While there, he visited the library, opera, and the famous Palmer House. Jonathan Hamilton Baker of Palo Pinto, Texas, drove his own cattle to Chicago and St. Louis. On one of his many trips, he brought back Palo Pinto County's first sewing machine.[11] After the Missouri-Kansas-Texas Railroad completed their lines into Texas, most cowboys hitched a ride back home on the train.

The progress that the cattle drives forged wrecked environmental havoc on the fragile ecosystem of the prairie. Buffalo hunters followed the trails, and the mass slaughter of these incredible animals changed the Plains forever, not to mention the Plains Indians' lives. The cows trampled meadows, the trains sliced through some of the best farm land in the territory and states, and industrialization quickly followed the cattle drives. Farms, cities, and mills soon rose up along the grasses and the Cross Timbers to compete with the wildlife. The Plains became permanently altered by the economic boom that resulted from the drives.

Cow Towns

The reputations of the frontier towns that established themselves along the trails helped to create cattle driving lore. The images of gunslingers, gamblers, prostitutes, and tough marshals living in dusty towns are seared into the collective American memory. One cannot help but wonder when passing through places with names like Hell's Half Acre in Fort Worth, the Border Queen town of Caldwell, or Boot Hill Cemetery in Dodge City, just how many murders and quasi-legal hangings occurred.

While the cow towns did see their fair share of criminal mayhem, by no means were they as unsafe as often thought In fact, even Ellsworth, Kansas, the cow town with the highest murder rate, was statistically safer than modern-day Dallas. However, when towns sprung up almost overnight to conduct commerce with the cowboys, unsavory characters soon followed, and opportunity did not just beckon for the business-minded.

Fort Griffin Flat, Texas was home to Doc Holliday and his girlfriend, Big Nose Kate, who fled to Dodge City after other suspicious characters uncovered a gambling ruse. Spanish Fort, Texas saw many a shootout in its saloons – on one Christmas morning, four men were shot dead in a drunken brawl.[12]

Stag Saloon in Fort Worth. Courtesy Fort Worth Public Library.

In general, however, respectable men and women sought to find their fortunes in the cattle trade, and while almost all of them welcomed risk, they did not do so foolhardily. Establishing saloons, cobbler shops, doctor's offices, trading posts, hotels, and brothels required a good business head and a keen eye for opportunity. The civic leaders of these towns tried to curb violence and the influx of "riff-raff," going so far as to ban anyone from carrying guns into town.[13]

The leaders of the towns had to promote their cities aggressively, since as the rail heads moved further west, new settlements competed with the older ones to lure the cattle drivers away. Ellsworth, Kansas, for example, bad-mouthed Abilene in newspaper accounts and in fliers distributed to Texas drovers. They claimed their town offered nicer accommodations and more lucrative prices for the cattle.

Though prostitution and gambling were legal, civic leaders did not want all that wantonness in their own backyards. The larger towns, like Fort Worth, Wichita, and Dodge City, established special vice zones to keep the bawdiness in check. Gunslinging sheriffs and marshals were hired to keep law and order in the town, though the exploits of people like Bat Masterson and Wild Bill Hickock have been greatly exaggerated over the years, often by the men themselves.

The towns and their citizens, the cattle drivers and their charges, and the Native Americans fighting to maintain their culture while adapting to a new one, created a unique environment. The southwestern cattle trails in the post Civil War period became a world unto itself. Though the trails were only active for about 30 years, they left a lasting impression not only on the history of the region, but on the very identity of America.

The End of the Trails

Though historians like to find the one overriding cause for the trails' demise, not one reason has achieved general consensus. Several factors contributed to the end of the cattle trails and their distinctive culture.

The earliest culprit was what farmers called "Texas fever." Southern longhorn carried a tick that gave other cattle an often fatal illness, but the longhorn themselves were immune. Farmers along the routes often forcibly stopped the Texas drives, and the Kansas legislature passed quarantine laws to curtail the devastating outbreaks. However, the quarantine laws were only haphazardly enforced because the cattle drives were so profitable.

Joseph McCoy, the very man who had established the Chisholm Trail, introduced another reason for the demise of the trails. McCoy was first and foremost a business man who invested heavily in improved cattle handling methods. He became a large shareholder in refrigerated rail cars, which allowed the shipment of slaughtered and processed cattle. After the railroad came to Denison, Texas in the 1870s, McCoy urged the use of local packing plants and refrigerated cars to ship beef more efficiently.[14] As shipping methods improved and rail heads proliferated in Texas, the need for the drives dwindled.

Towards the end of the trail drive era, outfits from Texas drove cattle north to stock the ranges in the Dakotas, Wyoming, and Montana. Soon, the herds on the ranches became self-sustaining, and influxes of Texas cattle were no longer needed.[15] Plus, America's palate was becoming more sophisticated, and the demand for longhorn beef – which was stringy and tough – declined drastically as wide-scale herd management led to better meat breeds.

An iconic symbol of the American West helped to undo cattle driving, too. Farmers used Joseph Glidden's invention of barbed wire to keep cattle off their land and away from their crops. Likewise, rich cattle ranchers did the same, stringing barbed wire to restrict other cattle's access to pastures and watering holes. Smaller ranchers, who had relied on the ancient tradition of open ranging, stood no chance against these property owners, even if these restrictions severely undermined the free market.

In Texas, a short but intense range war resulted as the old time cowboys clashed with the modern ranchers. Trail drivers cut the barbed wire to get to watering holes, but then had to contend with the rancher's buckshot. The Texas Rangers sided with the land owners, whose money and land holdings held powerful sway in Austin.

The old trail drivers were not without their own representation, however. As Indian Territory had begun filling up with white settlers following the Land Rushes, Texas and Kansas cattlemen formed the Cherokee Strip Livestock Association to make sure they retained access to the territory's rich grazing lands in the western section of the Cherokee Nation. But the U.S. government, bankers, railroaders, and real estate speculators saw other uses for the land. Claiming that the Cherokee Strip actually belonged to the U.S. government as a stipulation of the 1866 Reconstruction Treaty, President Grant's administration forced the Cherokee Strip Livestock Association to disband. The federal government claimed the "Cherokee Strip" and subsequently opened it to the Oklahoma land rush.[16]

In Washington, cattlemen had one last recourse. The U.S. Secretary of the Treasury, Hugh McCulloch, under the recommendations of former trail drivers, proposed that the government set aside a six mile wide stretch of land that would pass through Indian Territory, Kansas, and Nebraska and stop in the Dakota Territory. Naming it a "National Cattle Road," this proposed "cattle highway" had three purposes. First, the cowboys wanted to ensure that that the open range tradition remained. Secondly, representatives from the states and territories affected wanted to continue the cattle trade and its resulting prosperity. Lastly, Mr. McCulloch made the case that the cattle money received by the tribes in Indian Territory helped to make them more financially independent, which decreased their need for assistance from the U.S. Government. That this proposal did not receive much support in Congress attested to the situation in which the old cowboys found themselves: their way of life was quickly coming to an end.

Paradoxically, the most powerful culprit in the cattle drives' demise was the railroad. The federal government gave the Missouri-Kansas-Texas Railroad (the M-K-T) the right to become the first railroad to enter Texas from the north, and other charters soon followed. The M-K-T, the St. Louis and San Francisco Railway, the Chicago and Rock Island Railroad, and the Gulf, Colorado, and Santa Fe Railroad replaced the cattle trails from Texas to Kansas.

Like the cattle trails, railroads found themselves antiquated when automobiles began to dominate transportation. Roads, built alongside the tracks, replaced most railroad routes. Because the roads followed the tracks just as the tracks followed the trails, the highways of today now parallel the old cattle roads. Though the modes of transport have changed over the course of 140 years, the routes have not.

The modern era, with its steam powered machines, consolidated and concentrated wealth, and mechanization of human labor, ensured that the cattle trails would become relics of a distant past.

The Trails Today

Driving today's highways from Texas to Kansas through Oklahoma, one would be hard pressed to find evidence of the old cattle trails. Decades of plowing, grazing, razing, and concreting have replaced worn footpaths and rutted hillsides. Despite all the things that have been erased, however, some memory of the trails lives on. The hooves of millions of cattle left swaths of bald land on which prairie grass, however hardy, simply cannot grow.

Many people who knew the trail intimately either moved away, or moved on. The ways of the cowboy became just another outmoded anecdote or were romanticized in dime novels. Because Americans were increasingly moving to the cities, the West became "old" quickly.

Two efforts by two very different men helped to change that: George Saunders, famous cattleman and president of the Old Time Trail Driver's Association, and, oddly enough, Franklin D. Roosevelt.

Dugan wagon yard in Fort Worth. Courtesy Fort Worth Public Library.

In 1917, Saunders proposed to publish a compilation of trail drive histories from a portion of the estimated 35,000 men who had made the journeys. After much trouble, he persuaded J. Marvin Hunter, a newspaper reporter, to finish the project. Published in a very limited run in 1924, *The Trail Drivers of Texas* has become one of the most important sources for all cattle trail researchers. The book also helped to establish Texas as the quintessential trail and cowboy state, whether deserved or not.

During the Great Depression, with thousands of teachers, artists, and writers out of work, Franklin D. Roosevelt authorized the Federal Writer's Project (FWP) to give them something to do. Luckily for generations of Americans to come, the FWP, a subdivision of the Works Progress Administration (WPA), decided that the mission of the agency was to preserve American culture. The FWP sent out an army of intellectuals whose job was to gather interviews, songs, poems, photos, stories, histories, and information on the farms, towns, and states in all of America. The writers who traveled to Texas, Oklahoma, and Kansas recorded cowboy songs and transcribed the histories of trail drivers and Indians. Preserved through WPA Guides to the states and in manuscripts housed at the Library of Congress, this wonderful project – which was suggested to Roosevelt as an afterthought – created a rare collection of authentic voices that influence historians to this day.

Bob Klemme of Enid, Oklahoma, is one of those historians. In the 1990s, he proposed establishing the Chisholm Trail Heritage Highway to the Oklahoma Legislature, which unanimously agreed to dedicate US Highway 81 to the Chisholm Trail. Communities and cities along the trail marked it with white concrete trail markers at road intersections, and several cities began commemorating the trail with annual round-ups, reenactments, and festivals. In the ensuing years, Klemme's markers have been added to trail sites in Texas and Kansas, and even the Great Western Trail has been marked. In 2009, cities and towns that hug the path of the Shawnee Trail also began to erect commemorative markers. Local historians are lobbying the National Park Service to preserve the cattle trails in a national trail system.

Following the old cattle trails makes for an excellent driving vacation. You can step back through time to witness not only American cultural history, but American transportation and technological history by simply following the markers (and then veering from them to learn even more history!) American society formed along the trails, and its continued progression – always dynamic in a country that values immigration, innovation, and change – can still be seen today.

Chapter Two

FOLLOWING THE SHAWNEE (TEXAS) TRAIL

Carpenter Bluff's Bridge near Dension, Texas. Photo by author.

The first known long-distance trail in Texas that sent longhorns to their doom was the Shawnee Trail, so named because it may have bisected a Shawnee village at one point.[17] Contrary to the latter trails, the Shawnee Trail was not founded by any one person. Instead, cowboys simply followed a tradition of commercial interactions that had been established by Native Americans who used this path for inter-tribal trading and buffalo hunting expeditions.

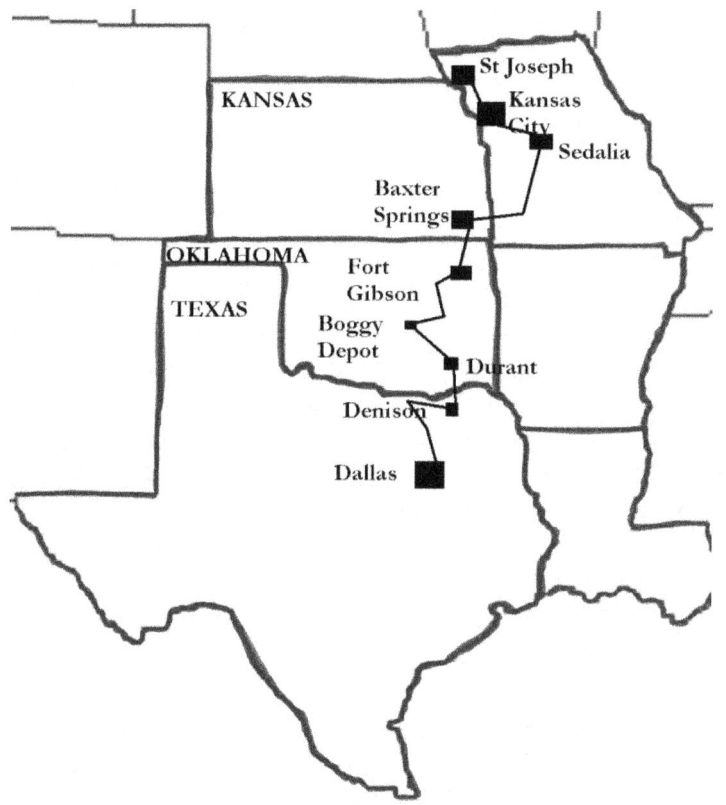

The old Shawnee Trail is far from linear.

Used as a cattle trail in the decades before and after the Civil War, various feeder trails met up at the Holland Coffee Trading Post at Preston, Texas before heading north through the Choctaw and Chickasaw nations. The trail then passed by Fort Washita, which was established in 1842. Trail hands bought supplies in Boggy Depot, then made their way around the Fort Gibson area and through the Cherokee nation before entering southeastern Kansas and southwestern Missouri. The cowboys either sold their cattle to middlemen in St. Joseph or Sedalia, Missouri or drove all the way to St. Louis or Chicago, where the stockyards and slaughter houses became the final destination for road-weary longhorn.

While the Shawnee Trail was actually the longest-lasting trail, it was geographically the worst. Cutting through the heart of fertile farm land, the drivers met with pioneers, wandering tribes, and goods traders traveling in every direction in search of land and opportunity to call their own, making the trail a bit over- populated. In addition, farmers in Indian Territory, Kansas, and Missouri resented the intrusion of the Texas cattle. The longhorns not only destroyed their crops but also hurt the farmers' own herds, especially when they brought in "Texas fever," a debilitating sickness that spread quickly among imported cattle and often led to death. By the 1870s, railroads usurped the Shawnee Trail. Eventually a more westerly route was needed, and drovers began to follow the Chisholm Trail.

The Shawnee Trail followed two roads: the earliest took an easterly course though Indian Territory all the way to Sedalia, Missouri. As sedentary pioneers and regional conflicts crowded out the old Shawnee Trail, drivers forged a new one that cut through the center of Indian Territory and drew a swath through Kansas before stopping at the railhead in St. Joseph, Missouri. When Kansas City became a major stockyard and slaughter center, some drivers sold their stock directly to the processing centers, if the price was right.

Of the three trails in this book, the Shawnee Trail will be the most "haphazard" tour, as its age, conflicted past, and loss of significance over the years have taken a toll on its history.

Cities and towns with amenities such as hotels, gas stations, and restaurants are marked for your convenience. Make sure to bring a detailed map with you as you drive along the Shawnee Trail!

Texas Shawnee Trail Tour (1 day)
Dallas, Plano, Frisco, Prosper, Celina, Gunter, Dorchester, Sherman, Pottsboro, Preston, Grandpappy Point, Denison

Texas is known the world over for being cow country, and its reputation began early. The longhorns were Spanish hybrids that roamed the vast lands around the Rio Grande Valley due to the lack of fencing. Cattle companies gathered herds of feral cattle – sometimes by roping, often by buying up cattle that other cowboys had roped – and then drove them to Galveston or New Orleans. From there, the cows were shipped up-river to St. Louis. This was a tough route, however, as the cattle had to wade through swamps, cross wide rivers, push their way through bramble thickets, and find forage in dark, piney forests.

As markets began to open west of St. Louis, Texas drovers realized that driving may be easier with an overland route. Cattle drives began shifting to the northeast, using old Indian, pioneer, and buffalo trails. The drives passed through San Antonio, Austin, Round Rock, and Waco (see Chisholm Trail for these stops), and then veered towards a small but busy village named Dallas.

Dallas
- Pioneer Plaza and Pioneer Cemetery
- Hotels, gas stations, and restaurants

Directions:
You will begin your tour at the intersection of Young and Griffin Streets in downtown Dallas. Pioneer Plaza is located near the convention center and city hall.

What's to See:
Dallas began as a trading post along a river crossing not far from Bird's Fort in what is now northern Tarrant County, which was a garrison built for pioneer protection. John Neeley Bryan, a young Tennessee lawyer, decided a high bluff along the Trinity River would blossom into a nice town and boasted about this perfect spot to all who would listen and read letters that he sent back home to Tennessee. Settlers began arriving to check out this veritable wonderland, but found just a grove of cottonwoods along the banks of a narrow but deep river. Somehow, the prairie seemed

to have beckoned even the most resistant, and within the first ten years of Bryan's trading post, Dallas had begun to form.

Pioneer Plaza in downtown Dallas. Photo by author.

Today, Dallas is a huge metropolis. The city grew to its size because of its location as a spring-fed fresh water source and trading crossroad. Early on, Dallas served as a buffalo hide trading center and leather processor, and after the Civil War, the city became a cotton shipping magnet. In the 1870s, Dallas became the fist spot in Texas where two railroads intersected, which guaranteed this bustling town on a prairie a strong future.

The approximate location of the Shawnee Trail is today's Oak Lawn Avenue, which runs on the western side of downtown. Cattle stopped at the Cedar Springs watering hole, and bedded down around the Trinity River. North of downtown, Oak Lawn Avenue becomes Preston Road.

While Dallas was never a true trail town in the modern sense of the phrase, the city commemorates the Shawnee Trail with beautiful bronze statues of life size horses, cowboys, and longhorns crossing a stream at Pioneer Plaza, situated in front of the Dallas Convention Center. Next to the park sits the neglected Old Settler's Cemetery, in which many prominent Dallasites have been laid to rest.

Plano
- Downtown Area
- Hotels, gas stations, and restaurants

Directions:
1) From Pioneer Plaza in downtown Dallas, take Young Street left (west).
2) Turn right (north) onto Griffin Street.
3) Turn left (west) onto Elm Street.
4) You will pass Dealy Plaza and the School Book Depository, from where President Kennedy was shot. An "X" in the road marks the fatal spot.
5) Continue on Elm Street as it merges into Commerce Street after the Triple Underpass.
6) Turn right (north) onto Riverfront Boulevard (formerly Industrial Boulevard). This road will parallel the Trinity River.
7) Turn right (northeast) onto Oak Lawn Avenue.
8) Continue north on Oak Lawn Avenue. North of downtown, Oak Lawn Avenue turns into Preston Road (TX 289).
9) Preston Road will take you through Highland Park, Far North Dallas, and then Plano.
9) After approximately 20 miles, you will enter the western portions of Plano.
10) To get to downtown Plano, turn right (east) onto West Plano Parkway.
11) Turn left (northeast) onto 15th Street and follow it for approximately 5 miles into downtown Plano.

What's to See:

Riverfront Boulevard, once known as Industrial Boulevard, is nestled against the Trinity River levees and was once Dallas' main business artery. Oak Lawn/ Preston Road, arguably the oldest road in North Texas, was named after Preston, an early trading center on the Red River and an important cattle trail crossing.

An early settlement of the Peters Colony, Plano began life in the 1840s as a trading post. The influx of railroads helped the little town grow; by the 1870s, Plano had been incorporated. The town stayed relatively small until the 1980s, when it grew into one of the largest suburbs in the nation.

The Shawnee Trail followed Preston Road, which sits in the annexed, far western portion of Plano, away from the city's center.

While the city, therefore, cannot lay claim to a first-hand cattle drive experience, it is still worth a visit for its charming downtown full of restaurants, bars, shops, and inter-city rail. Make sure to visit the Interurban Museum (901 E 15th Street), which pays homage to a long-distance street car system that connected Denison to Waco during the first half of the 20th century.

Frisco
- Statues and Heritage Center
- Hotels, gas stations, restaurants

Directions:
1) From downtown Plano, backtrack to Preston Road by taking 15th Street west.
2) Continue on 15th Street until it intersects with Plano Parkway. Turn right (west) onto Plano Parkway.
3) Turn right (north) onto Preston Road/ TX 289.
4) Follow Preston Road north for approximately 10 miles to Main Street in Frisco.
5) Turn left onto Main Street, which will take you to downtown Frisco.

What's to See:

While the St. Louis & San Francisco Railroad (the "Frisco") founded Frisco, the town actually got its start much earlier. Prior to the Civil War, the little town of Lebanon, just south of Frisco's city center, served as a trading post and stage coach stop. When the Frisco Railway built a lake and laid tracks to the east, Lebanon's residents just upped and moved many of their buildings to form a new town. Originally called Emerson, the town re-christened itself to Frisco in honor of the railroad.

Frisco remained a tiny town for several decades until it got caught up in the building boom brought on by rapid suburban growth in nearby Plano in the late 1990s. Seemingly overnight, Frisco exploded into a town of close to 100,000 people.

Most of Frisco's architecture is new today, though it does boast a charming downtown with many restaurants and galleries. South of Main Street is "Old Frisco," where an outdoor museum marks the Frisco Heritage Museum (6455 Page Street). At times, the museum exhibits an excellent re-telling of the Shawnee Trail, and also celebrates "Shawnee Trail Days" every April. Nearby are a science museum and the proposed site of the Museum of the American Railroad, with a tentative opening date of Fall 2011 (Cotton Gin Road). Don't miss the old calaboose on First Street. [18]

Prosper, Celina, and Gunter
- Downtowns
- Gas stations and restaurants

Directions:
1) From Main Street in Frisco, go east back to Preston Road/ TX 289.
2) Turn left (north) onto Preston Road/ TX 289 and follow it past US 380. North of US 380 are (in order) Prosper, Celina, and Gunter.

What's to See:

Considering the history of suburban expansion in the area, these towns are destined to grow like Plano and Frisco. For now, though, they retain a small-town feel.

The Frisco Railway founded Prosper. Residents from nearby Rock Hill (ca. four miles north of Frisco on Preston Road), a trail town founded in the 1850s, abandoned the settlement in favor of Prosper. Downtown Prosper can be visited by taking Business SH 289.

Celina dates back to the 1870s, but grew up around the Frisco railroad in the early 20th century. Celina's downtown along Business SH 289 is worth a visit, with many shops, restaurants, a visitor's center, and a small museum.

Gunter is the first town you'll pass in southern Grayson County. A true child of the Frisco railroad, Gunter was established in the early 20th century and named after a prominent cattleman, John Gunter. Gunter used to be so small that its high school offered scholarships to all of its graduating seniors. However, that tradition had to be discontinued as more people moved to the district.

As you drive up this ancient road, you'll notice the gentle contouring of the prairie landscape. Wider vistas beckon just to the west, making for spectacular sunsets. Early travelers waxed poetic about this countryside, and even today, it's not difficult to see why.

Dorchester
- Old Preston Road

Directions:
1) Approximately 2 miles north of Gunter on Preston Road /TX 289, take Strawn Road (gravel road) to the right (east).
2) Follow Strawn Road east and then north as it travels alongside the old Frisco track route, now used by the Burlington Northern Santa Fe.
3) After approximately 1.5 miles on Strawn Road, you'll come to the intersection of Strawn and Old Preston. Turn left (north) onto Old Preston Road. You are now on an original stretch of the Shawnee Trail.
4) Follow Old Preston Road until it bisects with Mackey Road. Turn left (north) onto Mackey Road and follow it to FM 902 in Dorchester.
5) At the intersection of FM 902 and Mackey Road, turn left (west) onto FM 902 into Dorchester. Across the tracks to the left lie the remains of Dorchester's downtown.

What's to See:
Dorchester, named after a local banker, had its start when the Frisco Railway came through. While the tracks still remain in use today, Dorchester's schools and main business district have closed. The old lake that supplied water to the Frisco rail line sits just south of the downtown, next to a defunct water tower, which was also the site of Dorchester's long-gone depot.

Dorchester's downtown has seen better days. Photo by author.

Sherman
- Red River Historical Museum and railroad history
- Hotels, gas stations, and restaurants

Directions:
1) Follow FM 902 in Dorchester west to the intersection with Preston Road / TX 289.
2) Turn right (north) onto Preston Road / TX 289. Continue north on Preston Road / TX 289 for approximately 13 miles to the intersection of TX 289 and TX 56.
2) Turn right (east) onto TX 56.
3) Follow TX 56 east for approximately 5 miles into downtown Sherman. In downtown Sherman, TX 56 becomes Lamar Street.

What's to See:

When you follow TX 56 into Sherman, you will be on what locals call the "Marcy Road," named after Randalph B. Marcy, an Army captain who forged several trails (including this road) in the Red River Valley and also mapped the headwaters of the river in Palo Duro Canyon.

Sherman, established in the 1850s, is the Grayson County seat and is home to the Red River Historical Museum (301 South Walnut). The museum resides in a Carnegie Library, which sports Depression-era murals by artist James Swann. A prominent stop on the old Butterfield Overland Trail (1858-1861), Sherman is also a very railroad-oriented town. Its original 1888 Cotton Belt (St. Louis Southwestern Railway) depot, made of brick, sits just east of the downtown square on Lamar Street.

Interestingly, Sherman had to struggle to convince a railroad to come through its center. The town's fathers apparently did not entice the Missouri-Kansas-Texas Railroad (M-K-T) enough to make it the first stop in Texas; instead, the railroad just laid out the new town of Denison, north of Sherman. However, when the Houston and Texas Central arrived in Sherman from the south, the M-K-T finally extended its line south into Sherman.

To follow the original Preston Trail/ Shawnee Trail north of Sherman, you will need to travel Travis Street, which runs north/south on the east side of the courthouse square.

Preston Bend
- Cemetery

Directions:
1) From Lamar Street at the downtown Sherman square, take North Travis Street/ FM 131 to the north.
2) Continue traveling north on North Travis Street. After the intersection with Grayson Drive, North Travis Street turns into Preston Road. This is the original trail, as well as a portion of the Butterfield Overland Stagecoach route. Continue driving north on Preston Road.
3) Preston Road will intersect at FM 120. Turn left (west) onto FM 120 towards Pottsboro.
6) Follow FM 120 as it veers north of Pottsboro towards Lake Texoma.
7) Continue north on FM 120 for approximately 15 miles to Preston Bend. You will pass Preston Bend Park (private) and follow FM 120/ Preston Bend Road onto a peninsula.
8) At the "T," turn right to continue to Preston Bend. The cemetery will be on your right.

What's to See:

The M-K-T founded Pottsboro when tracks were extended to the west of Denison. Today, Pottsboro is a resort town for those who like to live around Lake Texoma.

The cattle on the Shawnee Trail did not trample through the town of Preston, though the cowboys did supply themselves at the Holland Coffee Trading Post, located near the center of town. The drives crossed the Red River at Rocky Point (also called Rock Bluff), a bit further east of Preston, between the town and Colbert's ferry landing.

Though Preston figured prominently in Texas history, it does not exist anymore. When Sam Rayburn, the longest running Speaker of the U.S. House of Representatives and a Bonham, Texas native, authorized the building of Lake Texoma in the 1940s, Preston became one of the lake's unfortunate drowning victims.

Though Preston is now under water, its cemetery remains. You can visit the grave of Holland Coffee, the owner of the trading post and one of Sophia Suttenfield's four husbands. Sophia proved to be one of Texas' most interesting women. She supposedly nursed Sam Houston during the battle of San Jacinto. Her second husband, Holland Coffee, lobbied to get her first marriage to Jesse Aughinbaugh annulled after he had gone missing for several years. Coffee and Sophia Suttenfield-Aughinbaugh married and moved to the trading post in Preston, where they built Glen Eden, one of the earliest plantations along the Red River. After Coffee was murdered in 1846, Major George N. Butt married Sophia Suttenfield-Aughinbaugh-Coffee, but he was killed in 1863 by members of Quantrill's Raiders. During the Civil War, Sophia gained fame as a fearless confederate who crossed the Red River by moonlight to warn Colonel James G. Bourland that Union soldiers had commandeered Glen Eden. In 1865, Sophia married Judge James Porter, who lived with her at the plantation until he died. Sophia Suttenfield-Aughinbaugh-Coffee-Butt-Porter died in 1897, and her grave lies buried in the Preston cemetery next to Holland Coffee.

The cemetery is all that remains of Preston. Photo by author.

To save Sophia's famous home, Glen Eden, from the oncoming waters of Lake Texoma, historians from the open-air museum Loy Lake Park (Loy Lake Road on US 75 between Denison and Sherman) moved the structure to the park. Unfortunately, the timbers of the dismantled home were accidentally burned and destroyed. Some usable remnants were repurposed for rebuilding other historic homes inside the museum.

Grandpappy Point
- Rocky Point, Shawnee Trail Crossing
- Restaurant (seasonal)

Directions:
1) From the cemetery, backtrack south to Pottsboro on FM 120.
2) Turn left (east) onto FM 120 towards Denison.
3) Turn left (north) onto old Preston Road. This is the northern continuation of the road you previously traveled from Sherman.
4) Follow Old Preston Road for approximately 4 miles until it intersects with FM 84/ Texoma Drive.
5) Turn left (north) onto FM 84/Texoma Drive towards Grandpappy Point, a restaurant, marina, vacation lodge, RV park, and resort.
6) FM 84 will turn into Pappy's Road.
7) Less than a mile from where FM 84 turns into Pappy's Road, to the left (west) you will see a steep decline into Lake Texoma, where a number of boats are moored.

What's to See:

The steep hill that empties into Lake Texoma is considered the "natural chute" from which cattle were forded into the Red River while driving up the Shawnee Trail. Alternately called "Rocky Point," "Rocky Bluff" or "Rock Crossing," this steep hill still shows abuse from the thousands of hooves that made their way into the river.

While it's hard to tell due to the amount of land Lake Texoma has now claimed, the site of Holland Coffee's trading fort lies directly north of the bluff.

Grandpappy Point's restaurant is closed during the winter months, though it does host concerts and Christmas displays in December.

Denison
- Missouri-Kansas-Texas Railway headquarters, Eisenhower's Birthplace, and Carpenter's Bluff
- Hotels, gas stations, and restaurants

Directions:
1) From Grandpappy Point, backtrack south onto FM 84/ Texoma Drive.

2) Follow FM 84/ Texoma Drive southeast for approximately 7 miles until it intersects with TX 91.
3) Turn right (south) onto TX 91 to follow it for approximately 4 miles into Denison.
4) Turn right (south) where Tone Street meets TX 91 across from Texoma Medical Center. TX 91 continues on Tone Street.
5) Continue south on TX 91/ Tone Street until it bends east into Main Street.
6) Follow Main Street east into downtown Denison.

What's to See:

The Missouri-Kansas-Texas Railroad built Denison for its own use as the seat of its Texas charter. The M-K-T tracks, laid in 1872, were the first ones to link St. Louis with Texas. Denison also has a Chisholm Trail connection. Joseph McCoy, the founder of the Chisholm Trail, partnered in a Denison rail car company in his later years. He urged cattle ranchers to forgo trail driving and make use of the refrigerated cars in which he had heavily invested.

During its heyday, Denison blossomed as the quintessential railroad town, with two large switching yards and a very active downtown. David Eisenhower, father of Dwight D. Eisenhower, worked for the M-K-T. The future president was born in a small, gabled house near the tracks, which now sits inside a state historical park (609 S. Lamar Ave).

Unfortunately, today Denison is just a shadow of its former self – the US 75 bypass has taken a lot of traffic off the main roads, and the many lines of track in the switching yards near downtown have been removed and sold for scrap. Ghosts of Denison's exciting past still linger, however. The downtown is home to many artists, wine tasting rooms,[19] and cultural endeavors. The former M-K-T headquarters houses the Red River Valley Railroad Museum (101 East Main Stret). Across the tracks from the museum is the ancient Traveler's Hotel, a three story, gothic mansion built by a German sea captain.

Of interest is the Carpenter Bluff's Bridge (approximately 10 miles east on FM 120), which spans the Red River between Texas and Oklahoma. Another relic of Denison's vast railroad history, this railroad truss bridge, which originally served the Missouri- Oklahoma- Gulf Railway, was converted for automobile traffic in the mid 20th century. Because of its narrow size, cars have to take turns crossing the bridge. Hugging the bridge is the "piggy back" section, which was used by pedestrians, buckboards, and early automobiles.

The Missouri-Kansas-Texas Railroad bridge between Texas and Oklahoma marks the Shawnee Trail crossing. Photo by author.

When you return to US 75/69 on your way out of Texas, stop by the Texas Travel Center on US 75, which offers maps and free coffee. Denison is a mere 10 miles from Oklahoma. Follow US 75 north and soon, you will cross alongside the multi-span, M-K-T truss bridge: you are now in Oklahoma, where the Shawnee Trail mirrors Native American history.

Oklahoma Shawnee Trail Tour (2 days)
Colbert, Durant, Fort Washita, Boggy Depot, Stringtown, Atoka, Kiowa, Pittsburg, McAlester, Robber's Cave, Porum, Checotah, Rentiesville, Muskogee, and Fort Gibson

The Shawnee Trail took many paths leading up north, so your journey will be more of a zig-zag than a straight line. As you enter Oklahoma, you also enter the Choctaw Nation, home to one of the Five Civilized Tribes who followed the Trail of Tears in the 1830s from their original lands along the Mississippi River into Indian Territory.

Oklahoma is the place where the South truly meets the West. While Oklahoma's history is chock full of intrigue and old West images, the southeastern part of the state still retains a very southern flavor. The Choctaws and Chickasaws who settled here after the Trail of Tears brought the plantation system with them, which included slaves. After the Civil War, white farmers from the South moved to Indian Territory in search of land and jobs, as did some of the West's most notorious outlaws. Freed slaves established towns in remote corners of the state. Ida Barnett Wells, the famous St. Louis muckraking journalist who exposed post-Civil War lynching, urged blacks to move into Indian Territory to seek better lives.

As these new settlers set up camp in Indian Territory after the Civil War, the railroad soon followed them. As part of the 1866 Peace Treaties with the United States, the nations in the eastern part of the territory were forced to cede millions of acres to the Missouri-Kanas-Texas Railroad. The Indian nations, however, successfully fought off the intrusion, but blatant attempts at land grabs continued. After Oklahoma statehood in 1907, these threats helped to create a forceful movement for social equality, which historians have termed "agrarian socialism." The Green Corn Rebellion of 1917 served as a good example of this attempted reform, as do the observations of Oklahoma's favorite son, Will Rogers.[20]

During the Shawnee Trail era, cattle drivers paid tolls to cross through Chickasaw, Choctaw, Creek, and Cherokee lands and spent weeks in the territory to let the cattle graze. The drivers also bought more cattle from Native American breeders to sell further north to ranchers and to the slaughter houses. The Cherokees especially were known for their superior cattle. Because the tribes in the eastern Indian Territory had been mostly acclimated to the white man's ways, Texas cattle drivers generally had uneventful crossings through the territory. The clash of cultures which later dominated the more westerly trails did not take place along the Shawnee Trail.

Colbert
- Red River ferry crossing
- Gas stations

Directions:
1) From the downtown Denison, turn north onto Eisenhower Parkway / US 69.

2) Follow Eisenhower Parkway/ US 69 north as it merges into US 75/ US 69.
3) You will cross the Red River on the US 75/ US 69 bridge into Oklahoma. Immediately upon crossing the bridge, turn right into a gravel parking lot, which sits beside the train tracks.
What's to See:

      The first town you'll meet on your journey north is Colbert, named after Benjamin Colbert, a man of Chickasaw descent who operated an important ferry that crossed the Red River. The location of the former ferry is about three miles east of the US 75 bridge (the pillars of the toll bridge, which Colbert would help erect, still stand down river).[21] A good historical vantage point of this important river crossing can be seen in a roadside parking lot next to the 1909 KATY truss bridge and immediately to your right as you cross over the US 75 bridge. Please note that the train tracks are active and private property and should not be crossed. Colbert also has an Oklahoma Travel Center, which offers maps and free coffee.

Durant
- Downtown, Three Valley Museum, and Large Peanut
- Hotels, gas stations, casinos, and restaurants

Directions:
1) From Colbert, continue north on US 75/ US 69 for approximately 15 miles to Durant.
2) Take the Main Street / US 70 exit right (east).
3) From the exit ramp, turn left (east) onto Main Street / US 70.
3) Follow Main Street / US 70 east for approximately 2 miles into downtown Durant.
What's to See:

      Durant began as a small trading post, but gained most of its prominence when the railroad came through in the 1870s. Durant is home to the World's Largest Peanut, a quite impressive statue on the Courthouse Square, or at least as impressive as far as concrete legumes go. Durant, named after Dixon Durant, a French-Choctaw pioneer and a Choctaw Chief, is today still an important center for the Lake Texoma region, and has a busy and friendly downtown. The Three Valley Museum, named after the Red River, Blue, and

Washita River Valleys, exhibits many artifacts pertaining to Bryan County history (401 East Main Street).

Fort Washita
- Fort Washita State Historic Park

Directions:
1) From Main Street in Durant, turn north onto North First Avenue/ OK 78/ OK 48.
2) Follow OK 78/ Ok 48 for approximately 6 miles.
2) Turn left (east) onto OK 78 when OK 78 and OK 48 split. Continue east on OK 78 for approximately 8 miles.
3) Turn left (east) onto OK 199.
4) Fort Washita will be on your right in less than a mile.

What's To See:

Fort Washita is in a state of arrested decay. Photo by author.

Though cattle trails never crossed onto military installations (too much damage could be sustained to the forts by the cattle's hooves) Fort Washita, built in 1842, is a contemporary of the Shawnee Trail, and is therefore important to include on this road trip. Built as a protective outpost after the Chickasaws moved onto their assigned lands, the fort's main function was as a staging area during the Mexican American War. Zachary Taylor commandeered a Fort Washita company, leading them through Texas on the still visible military road. The union army abandoned during the Civil War, and afterwards settlers dismantled the fort brick by brick to use in their own houses. The Colbert family, who ran Colbert's

Ferry, lived in one of the barracks at the fort until a fire gutted their home.

Cattle drivers and settlers both sought refuge inside forts from hostile people, such as Plains Indians, who fought the intrusion by the Indian nations onto their hunting and camping grounds.

Today, Fort Washita is a scenic ruin. The fort's gently sloping hills, ivy-covered ruins, remains of the Military Road and California Trail, and proximity to a Wild West heritage make it a destination for international as well as local travelers. The fort is also reputed to be haunted.

Boggy Depot
- Boggy Depot State Park

Directions:
1) From Fort Washita, turn left (west) onto OK 199 to backtrack to OK 78.
2) Turn left (north) onto OK 78.
3) Follow OK 78 north for approximately 9 miles to the intersection of OK 48.
4) Turn right (east) onto OK 48.
5) Follow OK 48 east for approximately 10 miles to Coleman.
6) In Coleman, turn right (east) onto 5th Street, then turn left (northwest) onto Grand Street. Grand Street will turn into Rock Creek Road/ E1890.
7) Continue driving northwest on Rock Creek Road/ E1890.
8) Turn left (north) onto Overland Trail. This is the old stage coach route into Boggy Depot.
9) Continue north on Overland Trail until it intersects with West Boggy Depot Road / E1870
10) Turn left (east) onto West Boggy Depot Road/ E1870 until it intersects with Park Lane.
11) Turn left (north) onto Park Lane (signs to the state park should direct you). After crossing Boggy Depot Creek, you will enter Boggy Depot State Park.

What's to See:

Today, the first capital of the Choctaw nation is a very small and very out-of-the-way state park, and nothing remains of the town except the cemetery and a few discernable foundations. A stop is in order, anyway, because the history of Boggy Depot is important to the history of Oklahoma, and who knows? You may find a ghost to two lurking here.

Nothing remains of Boggy Depot except the cemetery. Photo by author.

After the Chickasaws and Choctaws settled onto their assigned lands in the late 1830s, the first thing they did was to build a town with the amenities of the homes they left behind. Very quickly, Boggy Depot had a school, a Masonic Lodge, a church, and became a busy trading center. One of its main industries was in supplying bois d'arc seeds to farmers in Kansas, who used the strong, intertwining limbs of the trees to create hedge-row fences around their properties.

Boggy Depot was a main stop on the Shawnee Trail – one could say that the trail existed because of Boggy Depot. Chickasaw and Choctaw ranchers sold their cattle stock to the Texan trail drivers. The nation also charged tolls per head of cattle that trailed through their land, and operated a ferry across the Clear Boggy River.

In the 1850s, the Butterfield-Overland Stage Coach ran through Boggy Depot, where the coaches loaded up on supplies. The governor of the Chickasaw nation as well as the American liaison lived in the town, too.

A skirmish occurred in Boggy Depot during the Civil War, when union troops ambushed confederate soldiers, who were camped just outside of town.

Despite its prime location and importance to Indian Territory, Boggy Depot faded away when the Chickasaws set up a nation independent from the Choctaws, and left as the town lay within Choctaw boundaries. Later, the railroad bypassed the town, relegating it to a ghost town.

The town that was once an important trading center is now in a remote part of Atoka County accessible only by winding country roads. Boggy Depot lies inside a state park, with hiking trails, informational plaques, and a small museum inside park headquarters. The cemetery is eerie, nestled among large trees, with hand marked graves and dismantled walls.

Atoka, Stringtown, Kiowa, and Pittsburg
- Kiamichi Mountains and mining towns
- Gas stations and restaurants

Directions:
1) From Boggy Depot, continue north on Park Lane for approximately 4 miles until it intersects with OK 7.
2) Turn right (east) onto OK 7 towards Atoka.
3) In Atoka, turn left (north) onto US 75/69 and follow the highway north for approximately 10 miles to Stringtown.
4) In Stringtown, continue to follow US 69 north to Kiowa.
5) To get to Pittsburg, turn right (east) onto 8th street / OK 63 in Kiowa. Follow OK 63 east for approximately 3 miles to Pittsburg. The abandoned mine shafts and equipment lie further east of Pittsburg on OK 63.

What's to See:
From Atoka to McAlester, your path will parallel the old Missouri-Kansas-Texas Railroad tracks, which are now owned by Union Pacific. The road and the tracks mirror the paths of the military, Texas, and Shawnee Trails.

Atoka, an old Choctaw settlement, grew around Geary Station, where the Butterfield Overland Stagecoach stopped.

Stringtown owes its existence to farming, timber, and coal deposits. The granite marker that sits on the west side of US 69 tells of the time Clyde Barrow and Raymond Hamilton killed an Atoka County sheriff's deputy at a Stringtown dancehall.

Kiowa was founded by the Missouri-Kansas-Texas Railroad. Cattle pens used to line the tracks that run next to Harrison Street Avenue, or what was once the old Shawnee Trail. An interesting bee hive kiln sits next to an abandoned cotton gin on Van Buren Avenue near Kiowa's small downtown.

Ruins of coal mines sit in a farmer's field east of Pittsburg. Photo by author.

All that is left of Pittsburg, a coal-mining town that once held considerable wealth, are remnants of what used to be. A gymnasium is the original high school's lone survivor; abandoned mine shafts lie in fields; the tracks of two railroads have been sold for scrap; and most of the businesses are boarded up. At the turn of the 20th century, Pittsburg was the most prosperous town in the area. Now, with a population hovering around 200, it barely registers as a town at all.

McAlester
- Site of Perryville and Old Town
- Hotels, gas stations, restaurants

Directions:
1) From Pittsburg, backtrack west on OK 63 to US 69 in Kiowa.
2) In Kiowa, turn right (north) on US 69. Follow the highway for approximately 16 miles to McAlester.

3) Drive past the intersection of US 69 and the Indian Nation Turnpike. Turn left (west) onto Chambers Road / E1480, which is the first road to the left past the Turnpike bridge.
4) The site of old Perryville lies along Chambers Road between Cable and Parkhurst Roads.
7) To get to downtown McAlester, backtrack from old Perryville to US 69 and turn left (north) onto US 69.
8) Follow Business US 69, which becomes Main Street, into downtown McAlester.

What's to See:

As you drive north on US 69 into McAlester, you'd never guess from peering out your car window that you are traversing historic ground. Approximately four miles southwest of McAlester lies the old site of Perryville, once a very important city in Indian Territory. Founded by James Perry, this small town lay at the intersection of the military roads to Fort Washita, Fort Arbuckle, and Fort Smith, as well as the Texas Trail and the California Gold Rush Road as surveyed by Randolph B. Marcy. Perryville's location made it a very popular place – stage coaches as well as military camps set up shop here. In 1863, a civil war battle burned the town to the ground. When the Missouri-Kansas-Texas Railroad decided not to put a depot in Perryville, this busy crossroads died. It is now located near the McAlester airport along Chambers Road, where a few stone foundations remain hidden in the trees. The town site and battle field are listed on the National Register of Historic Places.

Coal that companies mined for the Missouri-Kansas-Texas Railroad, and the many international miners that came to McAlester to work in the mines, made McAlester the region's economic hub. McAlester is also home to Oklahoma's death row. The 1908 maximum security prison complex houses a small museum that exhibits the old electric chair (corner of Stonewall Avenue and West Street, west of Main Street/ US 69).

McAlester has a rich and vibrant history, as retold in the Krebs Heritage Museum (85 S. Main Street) and the old High School Museum (220 E. Adams). Make sure to visit McAlester's "Historic Old Town" district (North Main Street and Krebs Avenue), where you can find the first courthouse in McAlester (315

E. Krebs). Old cattle stockades that sit next to the railroad tracks are still visible in the Old Town district.

Wilburton
- Robber's Cave State Park
- Gas stations and restaurants

Directions:
1) From Main Street in downtown McAlester, turn east onto East Carl Albert Parkway / US 270/ OK 31/ OK 1.
2) Follow US 270/ OK 1 east out of McAlester for approximately 32 miles to Wilburton.
3) In Wilburton, turn left (north) onto OK 2.
4) Follow OK 2 for approximately 5 miles to the entrance of Robbers Cave State Park, which will be on your left. Follow signs to the cave.

What's to See:

Inside Robber's Cave. Photo by author.

Driving north, you will notice a gradual uplift of timbered and rocky hills. Within these mountains, secrets are hidden, as you will find in Robber's Cave State Park.

Robber's Cave, where Jesse and Frank James, Cole Younger, and Sam Starr once cooled their heels, is a state park inside the Choctaw nation. A considerable but do-able climb that the Civilian Conservation Corps marked with metal arrows in the

1930s takes the visitor to the cave, which actually consists of two stone slabs resting against each other. Generations of graffiti – including some entries from the late 19th century – provide a kind of "outlaw" flair. The park warns that people with health problems should not climb to the cave. Other activities and sights include a small lake, overnight camping, hiking, biking, and rock climbing.

Near Porum
- Belle Starr's Grave

Directions:
1) From the entrance of Robbers Cave State Park, turn left (north) onto OK 2 for approximately 19 miles.
2) Where OK 2 intersects with OK 31, turn left (west) to follow OK 31 into Quinton.
3) In Quinton, turn right (north) onto OK 71. Follow OK 71 for approximately 15 miles – you will cross over Eufaula Lake Dam.
4) Approximately 1.5 miles after crossing the dam on OK 71, you will see a dirt road on your left (this is the only dirt road to your left after the bend past the dam).
5) Turn left onto the dirt road, named Belle Starr Cemetery Road / D 1180 (may not be marked).
6) Follow the road until you get to a bed post gate. This is the entrance to Belle Starr's old homestead and grave (walking path). Depending on weather and maintenance conditions, the path to her grave may or may not be passable. Like Belle had to do so many years ago, proceed at your own risk!

What's to See:
     The landscape within this portion of the journey is quite picturesque. Scenes of forested hillsides cut by clear streams of an ancient mountain range will unfold before you.
     As you drive northeast towards Belle Starr's grave, you will enter into the Cherokee Nation. Having been expelled from their homeland in the foothills of Georgia and Tennessee, the Cherokees' new territory in what would become Oklahoma was not conducive to agriculture, and the Cherokees struggled for years to prosper again. The nation did find wealth in cattle, however. They traded cattle with Texans, charged tolls to allow the cattle to pass, and leased land in the western portions of their territory, which

helped the tribe to stave off the dreaded descent into "dirt farming."

Though the Cherokees had created well-organized governments with constitutions and laws, for many white ne'er-do-wells, the Quachita Forest (wah-shee-tah) appeared to be a bandit's haven. Because union soldiers stayed close to the forts and tribal police forces were mostly ineffectual, people like Jesse James and Belle Starr tended to "disappear" into the steep hills of the Cherokee Nation whenever trouble brewed. The forested ravines and stony outcroppings of the ranges proved to be good hideouts, too.

Belle's family was originally from Missouri; her brothers and first husband Jim Reed were members of Quantrill's Guerillas. With her second husband Sam Starr she owned a small farm in the Cherokee Nation of Indian Territory where the James and Young brothers hid out, and she herself could stay well away from the despised federal authorities. One of the most notorious female bandits of the Wild West, Belle Starr made her mark as a cattle and horse rustler. Instead of driving her ill-gotten animals to market, however, she sold them at stables she owned in Dallas and, later on, in Indian Territory.

Life was not easy for the "Bandit Queen:" her daughter became a prostitute, and her son may have had a hand in killing her, though that theory is still open for debate. She was shot off her horse as she was riding towards her farm, and her murder has yet to be solved.

Belle's grave lies in the front yard of what used to be her farm house. In 2007, an ice storm had obliterated the grave site, though as of this writing, it may be accessible once again. Her husband Sam Starr lies in the Starr Family cemetery south of Briartown on OK 2 (return to OK 70, continue east, turn south onto OK 2 to Briartown, turn east at the cemetery sign).

Finding Belle Starr's grave is an adventure in itself. Make sure you mark your path, or you might get stuck in the northern Oklahoma wilderness.

Checotah and Rentiesville
- Texas Trail and Civil War History
- Hotels, gas stations, and restaurants

Directions:
1) From Belle Starr Cemetery Road, backtrack to OK 70.
2) Turn left (east) onto OK 70.
3) Turn left (north) onto OK 2.
4) Follow OK 2 north through Porum for approximately 18 miles towards Warner.
5) In order to get back to the Shawnee Trail, turn left (west) onto US 266 just south of Warner. Follow this road for approximately 14 miles to Checotah.
6) In downtown Checotah, turn right (north) onto North Broadway Street/ Old US 69.
7) Follow North Broadway Street / Old US 69 north for approximately 3 miles to John Hope Franklin Road / E1030. Turn right (east) onto John Hope Franklin Road.
8) Follow John Hope Franklin Road into Rentiesville. Follow the signs in Rentiesville to the Honey Springs Battle site.
What's to See:

The Creek town of Checotah prospered from sitting at the intersections of the Texas Trail, Military Road, Shawnee Trail and later, the Missouri-Kansas-Texas Railroad. Most of Checotah's downtown district is on the National Register of Historic Places.

Northeast of Checotah is Rentiesville, a historically all-black town. After the Civil War, many freed African Americans sought a new life in Indian Territory, where they hoped to live as independently as possible from the whites. Many of these historic communities exist throughout Oklahoma.

The Honey Springs Battle Site, which commemorates the largest Civil War fought battle in Indian Territory, sits just east of Rentiesville. The site is marked with a walking trail explaining troop movement and Union victory. The Shawnee Trail is clearly visible at the battle ground.

Muskogee
- Historic downtown
- Hotels, gas stations, and restaurants

Directions:
1) From Rentiesville, backtrack to US 69. Follow US 69 north into Muskogee.
2) In Muskogee, turn right (east) onto Okmulgee Avenue/ US 64.

3) Follow Okmulgee Avenue / US 64 east for approximately one mile to downtown Muskogee.

What's to See:

Officially, Muskogee came into being when the Creek Nation allowed the Missouri-Kansas-Texas Railroad to locate a depot near the old Texas Trail. Soon, as home to the first bank in Indian Territory, Muskogee became the largest city in the Creek Nation.

The origination of the town occurred a little earlier than the railroad, though. Creek freedmen organized the first beginning of Muskogee. Soon thereafter, African, Native, and Anglo Americans moved here to take advantage of economic opportunities. The Federal Indian Bureau, the administration for Indian Territory, and even the Dawes Commission headquartered in the city as well. With this multi-cultural foundation, the city hosted the first and largest native heritage festival in the southwest for several years, which celebrated Indian food, traditions, and art.

Drivers going up the Shawnee Trail took an easterly course on what is today Okmulgee Avenue (US 64), then crossed the Arkansas River by ferry or on one of the only toll bridges in Indian Territory. The location of the ferries and the toll bridge, coupled with the proximity of Fort Gibson and the route of the Texas Trail, made the area around today's Muskogee an important trading center early on. Today, that trade continues at the city's inland port along the confluences of the Verdigris, Arkansas, and Neosho Rivers.

Muskogee is rightfully proud of its past. The Three Rivers Museum (220 Elgin Street), located inside a restored Midland Valley Railroad depot, pays homage to the city's history. The Five Civilized Tribes Museum (1101 Honor Heights Drive) celebrates the cultures and accomplishments of the Creeks, Seminoles, Cherokees, Chickasaws, and Choctaws inside the old 1875 Indian Agency building. Native American art is displayed at the Ataloa Lodge Museum on the Bacone College campus (2299 Old Bacone Road), and those interested in World War II can view the USS Batfish, a restored submarine, at the War Memorial Park and Museum (NE 48th Street and Water Plant Road). The Oklahoma Music Hall of Fame is located in Muskogee, too (401 South 3rd Street).

Fort Gibson
- Fort Gibson National Historic Landmark
- Gas stations, restaurants

Directions:
1) From downtown Muskogee, head north on Main Street / US 62 Business to Shawnee Avenue / US 62.
2) Turn right (east) onto Shawnee Avenue/ US 62 and follow it for approximately 5 miles to the intersection of N. Georgetown Road/ US 62 Business.
3) Turn left (north) onto US 62 Business follow this road to the town of Fort Gibson.
4) In Fort Gibson, turn left (north) onto Lee Street/ OK 80 and follow signs to the fort. You will pay entry fees at the old commissary/ museum/ park store.

What's to See:

Built in 1824 as an offshoot of Fort Smith, Arkansas Territory, Fort Gibson was the first federal military installation in what would become Oklahoma. The fort acted as a supply station, trading center, and hospital for Native American settlers. It was also the end-station for the Trail of Tears for the Cherokees, Creeks, and Seminoles. When these tribes came to the vicinity after the Indian Removal Act of 1830, Fort Gibson defended them against raids from hostile Plains tribes, like the Osages and Comanches.

Fort Gibson, situated along the Military Road that connected Indian Territory and Texas forts, also served as a staging area for western explorations. The Stokes Commission – a group of military men and adventurers hoping to make contact with nomadic Plains Indian Tribes – started off from the fort, as did several dragoon expeditions. The explorers recorded some of the first American encounters of Plains ecology and geography in diaries and journals, which eventually helped to open the area west of the fort for permanent settlement.

Early cattle drives skirted the fort on the eastern edge, away from the unknown territory to the West. As the Cherokees, Creeks, and Seminoles stabilized their nations, Shawnee Trail drivers came through their lands in order to trade, sell, and buy cattle.

The U.S. Army closed Fort Gibson in the 1850s after Cherokee complaints of "excess and wantonness" (translation: drinking and prostitution), but it was reopened during the Civil War as Fort Blunt, a union outpost. By the 1870s, the frontier had moved further west, and Fort Gibson was eventually abandoned. The buildings were either razed or re-purposed for other uses.

Fort Gibson's officer quarters. Photo by author.

The Works Progress Administration of the 1930s made Fort Gibson an extensive restoration project. The fort's wooden stockades were rebuilt around the parade grounds, though not in the correct location. Archeological digs have confirmed that the fort was located a little further west. The original stone buildings – officers' quarters, bakery, armory, commissary, and hospital – were stabilized or restored and sit east of the stockades, perched on a bluff with a beautiful view.

The National Historic Trust has designated Fort Gibson as a National Historic Site. Its museum, situated in the old commissary building across from the picturesque officer's quarters, offers plenty of information on the frontier settlers, but not so much on the cattle drives.

Kansas Shawnee Trail Tour (less than one day)
Baxter Springs

Fort Gibson was the last major stop in Oklahoma before the Shawnee Trail entered Kansas. Today, the route north of the fort is situated in an extensive mining area. One of these mining towns is Picher, Oklahoma which the Environmental Protection Agency declared uninhabitable in 2007 by the due to the level of lead found in the chat piles around town.

Many drovers came through Kansas on their way to Sedalia, St. Joseph, or Kansas City, Missouri. They tried to stay as far as possible from the "sod busters" in Missouri, but eventually, farming won out and pushed the trail west. Today, the area where the drovers trailed concentrates on industrial and agricultural activities. Therefore, we will not stay in Kansas for long, but the place we'll be visiting – Baxter Springs – is a quintessential old west town.

Baxter Springs – "First Cowtown in Kansas"
- Downtown, Baxter Springs National Cemetery, and Baxter Springs Heritage Center
- Hotels, gas stations, and restaurants

Directions:
1) From Fort Gibson, backtrack to Shawnee Avenue/ US 62 and follow it west into Muskogee.
2) Continue west on Shawnee Avenue/ US 62 for approximately 10 miles to the intersection of US 62 and US 69.
3) Turn right (north) onto US 69/ OK 2. Continue north on US 69 / OK 2 for approximately 57 miles to Vinita, Oklahoma.
4) In Vinita, follow US 69 as it merges with US 60 and OK 66 – also known as Route 66.
5) Follow US 69/ OK 66 through Afton, Narcissa, Miami, and Commerce, Oklahoma. Upon entering Kansas, you will drive into Baxter Springs.[22]
6) In Baxter Springs, US 69 becomes Military Avenue. Follow Military Avenue to downtown Baxter Springs.

What's to See:

Baxter Springs is named after – what else? – the springs found on someone named Baxter's property. It's picturesque village situated on the Kansas portion of Route 66. But its quaint façade hides its rather violent history - this is the area of "Bleeding Kansas."

In the 1850s, pro-slavery Missourians – among them the infamous William Quantrill - staged raids on abolitionist New Englanders who hoped to populate Kansas in large enough numbers to affect its admittance to the Union as a free state. At Fort Blair near the springs, General James Blunt and his men were killed in one of these raids in 1863, and are buried at the Baxter Springs National Cemetery.

After Missouri passed quarantine laws in the 1860s, Texas cattle drivers routed through Baxter Springs, where the town boosters built stockades. Because of the regional turmoil during the Civil War, drovers were often barred from moving further north and had to "hole up" in Baxter Springs, which depleted whatever profits they might have realized.

Baxter Springs sits along the fabled US 66. Photo by author.

Upon entering Baxter Springs, typical western entertainment awaited the drovers – gambling halls, saloons, and brothels. The town's location along the borders of Kansas, Indian Territory, and Missouri helped to foster its reputation for lawlessness. People in trouble with the law in one territory could hide out in the other, and loose themselves among the ramshackle mining camps within the Ozark piedmont.

Baxter Springs is located along the Kansas portion of Route 66. A restored Phillips gas station, built in 1929, serves as a Route 66 visitor's center and is part of the Baxter Springs Heritage Center (740 East Avenue). Victorian mansions reflecting both cattle driving and mining wealth are located throughout town.

Missouri Shawnee Trail Tour (2 days)
Sedalia, Kansas City, and St. Joseph

Missouri's Shawnee Trail history is sketchy at best. Cowboys decided where to drive their cattle based on the rates the railroads charged, and were often thwarted by Civil War inspired violence and by farmers who did not want some up-start cow nosing around their pastures. Hence, the two main stops for the Shawnee Trail, Sedalia and St. Joseph, were historically competitors with each other. St. Joseph's trail history wins out: as it sits right at the border of Kansas and not too far from Nebraska or Iowa, the town proved a draw not only for Texas drovers, but for forty-niners, Mormon pioneers, and stage coaches.

Many drovers called the Shawnee route the "Sedalia Trail" because they could meet up with the railroad in Sedalia. While not much evidence of the cattle drives remain, Sedalia still offers a fascinating look at life in the second half of the 19th century. An occasional glance is not justified for St. Joseph or Kansas City, either. St. Joseph is home to the Pony Express, Jesse James, and a very active Stockyards District. While due to its location, Kansas City is the second stop on our itinerary, it is actually the third Shawnee Trail site: it became a terminus after large packing houses located in the city's West Bottoms area. When the railroads came through, Kansas City became one of the most important beef processing centers in the country, usurping St. Joseph's dominance for many years. St. Joseph eventually got the upper hand, as its stockyards are still going strong, while the pens of Kansas City have succumbed to parking lots.

Sedalia
- Architecture, railroad history
- Hotels, gas stations, and restaurants

Directions:
1) From downtown Baxter Springs, take KS 166/ US 400 west to Interstate 44.
2) Follow Interstate 44 east for approximately 83 miles to Springfield.
3) In Springfield, take Exit 82 = US 65 and turn left (north) towards Fair Grove/ Buffalo/ Sedalia.
4) Continue north on US 65 for approximately 118 miles to Sedalia.
5) In Sedalia, US 65 intersects Main Street/ MO 765.

What's to See:

The Civil War halted the western expansion of regional railroads. Sedalia, as one of Missouri's western-most railheads before the conflict, was a Shawnee Trail terminus for several years. The town built stockades for the arriving drives, but had trouble keeping the drives coming as regional conflicts before, during, and after the Civil War prevented many drovers from getting to Sedalia.

Sedalia's boom occurred after the majority of the trail drives ceased – instead of a cow town, it became a railroad town, ferrying passengers to Kansas City or St. Louis on the Missouri-Kansas-Texas line. In the early 20th century, Scott Joplin, an African American pianist from Linden, Texas named his most famous piano composition, the Maple Leaf Rag, after a club in downtown Sedalia where he had worked from time to time. Joplin's ragtime music would come to define a whole era.

The Sedalia Area Chamber of Commerce offers an extensive tour through the architectural history of the town. Chief among the sites is the Missouri-Kansas-Texas station which houses the Visitor's Center (600 East Third Street). The M-K-T tracks have been converted to a hiking and biking trail. Sedalia also has a Carnegie Library that still serves its original purpose (3rd and Kentucky Avenue). Another not-to-be-missed building is the Missouri Trust Building (322 South Ohio Avenue). Its Romanesque turrets and gabled roofs recall a rare architectural period that mostly succumbed to the wrecking ball when gothic styling went out of favor by the 1900s.

Sedalia's heritage is readily apparent at the State Fair Grounds, where every year, exhibits from around the state are featured in several early 20th century brick buildings dedicated to agriculture, livestock, poultry, swine, and history (State Fair

Boulevard). Sedalia's Daum Museum of Contemporary Art (3201 West 16th Street) welcomes travelers who enjoy viewing art.

Kansas City
- West Bottoms and Stockyards
- Hotels, gas stations, restaurants

Directions:
1) From Sedalia, take US 50 west towards Kansas City. You will travel on this road for approximately 70 miles to Lee's Summit.
2) In Lee's Summit, turn left (west) onto I 470/US 50 and follow it for approximately 10 miles to the intersection of US 71.
3) Turn right (north) onto US 71 and follow it for approximately 14 miles to Kansas City.
4) At the southern edge of Kansas City, take Interstate Loop 670 to the west towards Kansas City, Kansas.
5) From Interstate Loop 670, take exit 1 B = Genessee Street. Turn left (south) onto Genessee Street to get to the Stockyards.
6) You are now in the West Bottoms stockyards district, which center around the Exchange Building at 1600 Genessee Street.

What's to See:

  Kansas City is on of the most mysterious and captivating cities in the nation. Mysterious, because so much unwritten, bloody history is contained here (the mobsters, the Kansas City Depot Job, and the political machines). Captivating (to cattle trail enthusiasts, anyway), because of the history of its original location, the West Bottoms.

  Sitting at the confluence of the Missouri and Kansas rivers, Kansas City began as a French settlement. The proximity to the Santa Fe Trail and later, the Oregon Trail, made Kansas City into a prominent trading post. John Calvin McCoy furthered trade by chartering supply barges from the east over the Missouri River to his port in Kansas City.

  During the early 1860s, drives bypassed Kansas City altogether as they headed east towards Sedalia, the western-most railhead at the time. It remained a small supply stop when cattle drovers passed through on their way to St. Joseph. Kansas City became a booming cow town only when the railroad came in 1869 and built a bridge across the Missouri River. But did it ever boom – by 1871 the stockyards, located at the state line between the Kansas

River to the west and the extensive rail yards to the east in what was called the West Bottoms, harbored stockades, exchanges, and became the birthplace of the world-famous culinary specialty, the Kansas City Steak. The Golden Ox restaurant, originator of the distinctively flavored steak, opened in 1949 and continues to operate in the original Stockyards Exchange building (1600 Genessee Street).

The Missouri and Kansas rivers defined Kansas City.
Courtesy Kansas City Public Library.

As with most stockyards, the location was not in the most genteel part of the city. Flooding in the West Bottoms was common, and the brothels, saloons, and gambling halls were legendary. North of the exchange, a red-brick warehouse district developed in the late 19th century. With the demise of the railroads in favor of interstate travel, the businesses of the stockyards and the warehouse district diminished greatly until the West Bottoms became akin to a ghost town.

Today, the West Bottoms are experiencing a renaissance of sorts. Artists and yuppies both have converted many of the warehouses into studios and lofts, and the former red light district is now home to the American Royals Convention Center. The wooden stockades are gone, and as of this writing, only the shell of a former slaughter house remains. Bike trails along the river offer great views of the West Bottoms warehouses, with their gothic beauty of industrial starkness.

Kansas City and its suburbs have a lot to offer its visitors. To locate the many attractions in Kansas City, request a brochure from the Kansas City Visitor's Bureau (see resources in the back of the book).

The Swift packing plant at the Kansas City Stockyards.
Courtesy Kansas City Public Library.

St. Joseph
- Pony Express, Jesse James House, and stockyards
- Hotels, gas stations, restaurants

Directions:
1) From Genessee Street in the West Bottoms in Kansas City, turn east onto the feeder road for Interstate 160 towards Topeka (follow signs).
2) Continue east to merge with Interstate 160.
3) At exit 2M, veer left (north) onto Interstate 70/ Interstate 35/ Interstate 29/ US 40/ US 71/ Bruce Watkins Expressway and continue north for approximately 3 miles.
4) At exit 2G, follow Interstate 35/ Interstate 29/ US 71 north towards the Kansas City International Airport and Platte City, Missouri.
5) At exit 1A, veer left (north) to follow Interstate 29/ US 71.
6) Follow Interstate 29/ US 71 north for approximately 60 miles to St. Joseph.
7) In St. Joseph, take exit 43 northwest to follow Interstate 229.

10) Exit at South 10th Street (one way) and go north into downtown St. Joseph.

What's to See:

St. Joseph is one of the true "western" towns. Home to Jesse James, the Pony Express, and still-active stockyards, this city, nestled amongst wooden hills along the Missouri River, embodies the original American West.

Like Kansas City, St. Joseph began as a French settlement, as it was situated at the eastern edge of Louisiana Territory. By 1826, Joseph Robidoux opened a trading post on what was called St. Michael's Prairie, and soon, other people began to populate this frontier town. Roughly twenty years later, St. Joseph experienced its first boom as a supply stop and trail head for the California Gold Rush seekers. Steamboats began ferrying passengers from St. Louis to St. Joseph over the Missouri River. The railroad came to the town in 1859, making it a destination for trail drivers as well. The apex of the drives, however, occurred after the Civil War, when the stockyards were built to handle the cattle. The stockyards were home to pens, processing plants, and tanneries, which are still in business today. Luckily for the noses of the citizens of St. Joseph, the stockyards are located downwind from town (MO 759/ South 2nd Street).

The Pony Express Stables now house a museum. Photo by author.

In 1860, the fabled Pony Express opened shop in a downtown stable. Its mail carriers traveled about 250 miles in one day, stopping at stations along the way to eat, change horses, and deliver or pick up mail. Though this romantic but unprofitable business lasted for only a year as the telegraph line reduced the need, its existence is still celebrated at the Pony Express Museum (914 Penn Street). The museum is housed in the original stables and offers interactive displays and a very interesting re-creation of the archeological dig of the stables.

Up the road from the Pony Express Stables sits another landmark of the true west: the Jesse James Home Museum (corner of Penn Street and Mitchell Avenue). This wooden, four- square house enshrines the last residence of the notorious outlaw, up to and including the furniture, pictures, and wall paper stains apparent on the day James was shot by Robert Ford in 1882. The bullet hole, directly underneath a cross-stitched, framed platitude of "Home Sweet Home," has been obliterated over the years by souvenir hunters who wanted an authentic piece of Jesse James plaster. Other authentic Jesse James memorabilia on display include pieces of his coffin, bone, a random bullet retrieved from his dead body, and a casting of Mr. James' skull. These rather macabre artifacts were unearthed after James descendants exhumed the body to conduct DNA testing to find out if the man buried under the name of Jesse James was the real Jesse James (he was).

Next to the Jesse James Home Museum is the Pattee House Museum (1202 Penn Street), which was once a hotel and stage coach stop. In its day, the huge Pattee House served as the most prominent building in St. Joseph, and today houses many artifacts from the western era such as a train, a stage coach, and even a real gallows.

End of the Shawnee Trail

Though the Shawnee Trail may be the oldest long-distance cattle trail in the southwest, its history is preserved the worst. The trail is mostly invisible, no museums are devoted to it, and only a few historical markers make mention of it. It's not nearly as well known as the next two trails you'll be driving. That should not stop you from retracing it, however. Once you know its history, the Shawnee Trail becomes just as fascinating as its western cousins.

Chapter Three

FOLLOWING THE CHISHOLM TRAIL

Monument Hill in Addington, Oklahoma. Photo by author.

Joseph McCoy (1837-1915), an Illinois cattle trader with unsentimental business acumen, described one of the last ill-fated cattle drives on the Shawnee Trail. He told of cattle drover James M. Dougherty who, upon entering Missouri, was ambushed by farmers who resented the cattle tearing up their fields. The famers tied Dougherty to a tree and severely lashed him. Left abandoned to his fate, with many of his animals stolen, Dougherty freed himself and eventually arrived in Sedalia, Missouri, but not without the impression that the Shawnee Trail had become too dangerous for cattle men.[23] This incident, McCoy wrote, led him on a journey to create a safer route for cattle trailing. The networks of roads he would later establish to drive cattle to market became known as the Chisholm Trail.

Because railroads had not yet built a network towards the south following the Civil War, cattle still had to be driven north to meet the trains. Therefore, McCoy had to persuade a railroad to establish a terminal further west than Missouri to move the cattle trade away from the farmers. He proposed the idea of creating a dedicated western cattle trail beyond the edge of "civilization" to the short distance carrier Hannibal and St. Joseph Railroad, which agreed to set up a terminal in the small dugout town of Abilene, Kansas.

With the first step secured, McCoy still had to figure out the route of his proposed road. Tim Hersey, surveyor and founder of Abilene, measured almost a straight line from Abilene south to the Kansas border for the new trail, part of which had been previously forged by Black Beaver, a Delaware guide and interpreter. Black Beaver had led Union troops out of Indian Territory during the war, as many citizens of the Indian Nations in Indian Territory had allied themselves with the Confederacy and had taken over federal forts.

In Indian Territory, Hersey's survey relied on a trail that had already been forged by a well respected goods dealer and interpreter, Jesse Chisholm. Jesse Chisholm was a Scots-Cherokee man whose dearest desire was to be left in peace. With his ability to speak five Indian languages as well as Spanish and English, read and write, and his good nature, not many people honored that wish.

He spent most of his life traveling from peace negotiations to trading posts and back, finding nothing but friends along the way.

Chisholm's trail was actually quite short, extending only from Kansas into the vicinity of Oklahoma City. Initially, Chisholm forged the road not for trading, but to help the Wichitas flee the threats of the Civil War in Indian Territory. Hersey extended this trail towards the southern end of the territory.

Upon establishing the route, McCoy traveled to Texas to convince cattle owners that a railhead existed specifically for the longhorn trade. He visited saloons and churches to get his message out. Relying on nothing but faith, Colonel O. W. Wheeler and his outfit took the "carpetbagger's" word and drove the first herd up the Chisholm Trail, numbering 35,000 head, in 1867.[24] After the outfit's safe and uneventful journey, more Texans followed suit.[25]

The original Chisholm Trail extended only from Kansas to northern Oklahoma.

The location of the actual Chisholm Trail still confuses many a historian. Two other "Chisholms" have competed in our collective memory as the trail's namesakes. Thornton Chisholm from Cuero, Texas, trailed his cattle in 1866 to St. Joseph, Missouri. His drive walked through Texas in a westerly direction on the "Old Beef Trail" (see Great Western Trail), cut a northeastern path through Indian Territory, then drove through Kansas to the stockyards in St. Joseph. Another contender is John Chisum, a cattle rancher from Tennessee who settled in Paris, Texas and later established a ranch in Denton County, Texas. He blazed his own "Chisum Trail" directly west from North Texas to a larger ranch in New Mexico.

The great numbers of men (and some women) who took McCoy's lead to trail cattle along the Chisholm Trail marked the emergence of a post-war boom economy. Soon, other towns in Kansas besides Abilene wanted to become the trail terminus, such as Ellsworth, which promoted itself as a better town conducive to both business and pleasure. Other towns grew more organically. Locals saw a ready market for supplying the outfits with food and gear, and small but active villages sprang up all along the Chisholm. Spanish Fort, Texas, for example, became *the* supply station for boots when H.J. Justin settled along the trail. The railroads later bypassed many of these way stations, and today they exist only as ghost towns.

Surprisingly, McCoy helped to undo his very own trail. By the late 1870s, he had started to invest in refrigerated rail cars. He moved to Denison, Texas to manage the Atlantic and Texas Refrigerating Company, of which he was part owner. To protect his new business, he promoted slaughtering cattle locally and shipping processed beef to markets via rail.

The new and booming railroad settlements along the trail enticed other settlers who were not interested in cattle trailing. Within ten years, farmers started to lay claim to the lands around the Chisholm Trail and run-ins between the cowboys and the so-called "sod busters" were common. Paying tolls to farmers in Indian Territory – most of whom were citizens of the Chickasaw, Cherokee or Choctaw nations- proved the most irksome practice for the cowboys. Soon, drovers started to look for a westerly route away from the farms, and they began taking the Great Western Trail.

Texas Chisholm Trail Tour 1 (2-3 days)
Lockhart, Austin, Round Rock, Georgetown, Salado, Belton, Waco, Meridian, Kimball, Cleburne, Fort Worth, Decatur, Bowie, Montague, Nocona, Spanish Fort, Red River Station and Ringgold

The Chisholm Trail never really existed in Texas, as Tim Hersey did not survey the route that far south. What Texans now call the Chisholm Trail is actually a network of unnamed feeder trails that converged either in Fort Worth or in Montague County. But who are we to argue with Texans?[26]

These feeder trails skirt around a perceptible divide in the landscape. East of the trails, Texas' topography is decidedly timbered and green. West of the trails, the landscape becomes scrubby, arid, and flat. This conversion zone marks the point where rainfall diminishes along the southern-most boundary of the Great Plains. Because the land did not seem to be suited permanent settlement, these trails proved an ideal conduit for the cattle trade during the Chisholm Trail's brief reign.

While the towns south of Fort Worth are part of the Chisholm Trail tour, they also served cattle drovers who took the more easterly Shawnee route.

Lockhart
- Downtown and Jail Museum
- Gas stations and restaurants

Directions:
Your journey will begin at the Caldwell County Courthouse in Lockhart at 110 South Main Street in downtown Lockhart. Lockhart sits along US 183 about 19 miles east of San Marcos, Texas and 31 miles southeast of Austin.

What's to See:
Lockhart historians claim that one of their townsmen was the first to drive cattle up the Chisholm Trail, as Colonel J.J. Meyers made the journey in 1868, and before him, Thornton Chisholm from Cuero, Texas, trailed through the town. Thus, Lockhart's association with the "Chisholm Trail" might be due to the

Thornton Chisholm's drive, which was independent from Joseph McCoy's surveyed trail. What has become known as the "Chisholm Trail" through Lockhart was actually a main feeder trail for various cattle roads and was at times called the "Old Beef Trail." The destinations varied, as well. Some drives went to St. Joseph, while others went east into Louisiana and to the Mississippi River. In any case, cattle driving became a major industry for Lockhart for several years, before cotton production made more economic sense.

Visit the museum inside the county jail. Photo by author.

Founded in the mid-19th century, Lockhart has grown into the sizable seat of Caldwell County. Today, most of its interesting architecture dates from the railroad period, which occurred after the Civil War. The imposing white stoned courthouse was built in 1894, and its gothic-style jail, which today houses the Caldwell County Museum (315 E. Market Street), was built in 1908. Proud of its western heritage, the city hosts a four-day Chisholm Trail extravaganza every June.

Austin
- Downtown, State Capitol, and Bob Bullock Museum
- Hotels, gas stations, and restaurants

Directions:
1) From Main Street in downtown Lockhart, take North Colorado Street / US 183 north.

2) Follow US 183 north to Mendoza.
3) Continue to follow US 183 into Austin. Once near Austin, US 183 becomes Lockhart Highway.
4) When US 183 / Lockhart Highway crosses the Colorado River, the road's name turns into Airport Freeway.
5) You will come to a jumble of roads, all intersecting each other. You will need to veer left (northeast) onto Cesar Chavez Boulevard/ East 1st Street, which will take you into downtown Austin.
6) Cesar Chavez Boulevard becomes a one-way street facing southwest at Brazos Street.
7) Turn right (north) onto Brazos Street. Follow this street to 2nd Avenue.
8) Turn left (west) onto 2nd Avenue.
9) 2nd Avenue will intersect with Congress Avenue. To get to the state capitol building and the Bob Bullock Museum, turn right onto Congress Avenue.

What's to See:

Just north of Mendoza, you will cross TX 21, known as the Camino Real de los Tejas. This is an ancient trading and military road network that the Spanish forged during colonial Texas, using old Indian trails. The Camino Real (King's Highway) links Natchitoches, Louisiana to Guerrero, Mexico. The road runs through Texas' oldest cities, such as San Augustine, Nacogdoches, San Marcos, and San Antonio. Further north on US 183, you will drive through the old settlement of Mustang Ridge, which once was a popular watering hole for cattle on the trails, and was also a stage coach stop during the latter half of the 19th century.

Austin, the capitol city of Texas, is worth a stay for several days, though that's not due to the cattle drives. Austin is simply a lovely town, full of parks, hiking paths, and wildlife, such as the Mexican free-tail bat colony underneath the Congress Avenue Bridge.

While cattle drivers, bosses, and investors traded in Austin, the cattle themselves stayed well east of the city. This was not only due to the sizable population of Austin in the post-Civil War period, but also because of the topography. To the west of the city, the Texas Hill Country climbs boldly out of the landscape, whereas the terrain is much smoother on the eastern side. Cowboys forded the Colorado River just east of today's McKinney Falls State Park and walked northwest along today's Interstate 35 into Round Rock.

The cattle drives are recalled in the Bob Bullock Museum (1800 North Congress Avenue), a large, inter-active, and entertaining museum that recounts Texas history. Just south of the museum is the imposing state capitol building, free for touring. The Texas State Library, with plenty of exhibits and some genealogical materials, sits just east of the capitol. With the University of Texas anchoring the northern end, the city's center is full of vibrant restaurants, quirky stores, innovative art galleries, and several tranquil parks. Make sure to stop by the old Driskill Hotel (604 Brazos Street), which was built in 1886 by Jesse Driskill, a noted Austin cattle baron. The Driskill, it has been said, makes the best steaks in Texas. As with all culinary claims, that may depend on whose tongue did the tasting.

Please note that Austin's traffic is notoriously awful, and weekday rush hours can be very taxing. Parking is not free anywhere in downtown Austin.

Round Rock
- Downtown, Old Town Round Rock, the Round Rock, and Sam Bass' Grave
- Hotels, gas stations, and restaurants

Directions:
1) From the Congress Avenue in downtown Austin, turn right (east) onto either Martin Luther King, Jr. Boulevard or 15th Avenue.
2) Turn left (north) onto the north-bound Interstate 35 feeder road.
3) Merge carefully onto Interstate 35 north and follow it for approximately 20 miles to Round Rock.
6) In Round Rock, take Exit 250 B = South Mays Street and turn right (northeast) onto South Mays Street.
7) Follow South Mays Street north to downtown Round Rock.

What's to See:
Round Rock may be considered just another Austin suburb, but that designation is severely lacking. If you drive through Round Rock on the Interstate, you might never realize what a fascinating history this very modern city actually has. Settled by Swedish pioneers, Round Rock served as a trading center for Indians, settlers, and cattle drivers.[27]

Round Rock's visitor center and museum (East Main Street) are located downtown inside an original Swedish pioneer homestead, directly across the street from the bank which Sam Bass, one of the more storied bandits in Western Lore, attempted to rob before he was gunned down. Round Rock's main attraction is "Old Town Round Rock" (from downtown Round Rock, follow Round Rock Road west past Interstate 35 E and turn right on Chisholm Trail Road). Chisholm Trail Road, which runs through the old town, is the actual cattle trail. Today, the paved road crosses Brushy Creek next to a large, circular rock, from which the city derives its name. Tracks of pioneer wagons have been encased in the hardened soil alongside the Round Rock and are still visible. Many of the stone buildings that abut the road are contemporaries from the cattle driving days. In the Round Rock Cemetery (Sam Bass Road), Sam Bass' grave is marked by a triangular tombstone along the western fence. A rare slave burial ground is also part of this historically important cemetery (follow Chisholm Trail Road north to Sam Bass Road, turn left onto Sam Bass Road, then turn right into the main gate of the cemetery).

The street that crosses the stream near the Round Rock marks the original cattle and pioneer road. Ancient wagon ruts are clearly visible. Photo by author.

Georgetown
- Downtown and Gabriel Park
- Hotels, gas stations, and restaurants

Directions:
1) From either downtown Round Rock, Chisholm Trail Road, or the Round Rock Cemetery, backtrack to Interstate 35 north.
2) Merge onto Interstate 35 north and follow it for approximately 10 miles to Georgetown.
3) In Georgetown, take Exit 261 = West University Avenue/ TX 29 and turn right (east) onto West University Avenue/ TX 29.
5) Follow West University Avenue/ TX 29 into downtown Georgetown.

What's to See:

Georgetown, home of Southwestern University, began as a cotton trading center. It remained prosperous in the tenuous years after the Civil War because feeder trails ran right through its downtown. The cattle crossed the South and North San Gabriel Rivers north of the town's center.

Georgetown's downtown is a wonderful treat for visitors. With shops, restaurants, museums, and art galleries, the city has a lot to offer. Several downtown festivals (including a Chisholm Trail Festival in September) help to celebrate Georgetown's heritage. The Williamson County Museum, housed in a renovated bank building, offers interactive exhibits and tours (716 S. Austin Avenue). San Gabriel Park (N. Austin Avenue) which centers on a spring-fed swimming hole, has been used for centuries by two and four legged creatures, including cattle going up the Chisholm Trail.

Salado
- Stagecoach Inn, river crossing, and Salado College ruins
- Hotels, gas stations, and restaurants

Directions:
1) From downtown Georgetown, take N. Austin Avenue north to Interstate 35.
2) Go north on Interstate 35 for 24 miles.
3) Take Exit 283 = FM 2268/ Salado/ Holland.
4) Keep north on the feeder road north past the intersection of FM 2268.

5) The service road makes a "Y;" keep to the right. This road turns into Salado's Main Street. Follow this road to downtown Salado.
What's to See:
Salado is a pin-neat village nestled directly at the old river crossing. The Stagecoach Inn, a relic from the cattle driving days, serves up good food, lodging, and plenty of atmosphere (401 S. Stagecoach Road). The scenic ruins of Salado College (Main Street) look out over the town. Cattle forded the shallow water crossing at Salado Creek near the Main Street bridge.

Belton
- Downtown and Bell County Museum
- Hotels, gas stations, and restaurants

Directions:
1) From downtown Salado, go north on Main Street to Royal Street.
2) Turn left (west) onto Royal Street.
3) Turn right (north) onto Interstate 35.
4) Follow Interstate 35 north for approximately 14 miles to Belton.
5) Take Exit 294 A = Central Avenue.
5) At the intersection after the exit, turn left (west) onto East Central Avenue/ FM 263.
6) Follow East Central Avenue / FM 263 into downtown Belton.
What's to See:
Belton, seat of Bell County, was established well before the Civil War. After the war, the cattle trail passed just east of town. The restored Courthouse is worth a visit, as is the nearby wooden Missouri-Kansas-Texas Railroad depot (East Central Avenue). The Bell County Museum retells the long history of the county and displays a beautiful Chisholm Trail Monument (201 N. Main Street). Nolan Creek, which runs through the downtown area, is the center of a scenic park.

Waco
- Suspension Bridge, Elm Street, 2nd Avenue, and Texas Rangers Museum
- Hotels, gas stations, and restaurants

Directions:

1) From downtown Belton, take Main Street / FM 317 north to East 6th Avenue/ FM 93.
2) Turn right (east) onto East 6th Avenue/ FM 93.
3) At the intersection with Interstate 35, turn left (north) to merge with Interstate 35. Follow this road for approximately 48 miles to Waco.
4) In Waco, take Exit 335A = North 4th Street/ FM 1637.
5) Turn left (west) onto North 4th Street/ FM 1637.
6) Follow North 4th Street/FM 1637 into downtown Waco.

What's to See:

    The Wacos, a tribe of Indians who had established villages along the banks of the Brazos River, gave the city its name. Several natural springs fed the region, which made it a pleasant and fertile settlement. The arrival of American and Cherokee settlers signaled the end to the Wacos, who, after a series of peace treaties of which Sam Houston was the author, merged with the Wichitas and were eventually expelled to Indian Territory. The Cherokees, who had followed Sam Houston into Texas, were themselves forced to move to Indian Territory by Texans.

    The town of Waco was formally founded in 1856 near George Torrey's trading post, centering a region of cotton plantations.

Waco's suspension bridge served as a model for the Brooklyn Bridge. Photo by author.

After the Civil War, a large feeder trail crossed the river just east of downtown. In 1869, the city opened a suspension bridge across the river, which brought tolls and many more settlers to the area. The trail boss and the cook also crossed this bridge, leaving the drovers to help the cattle across the Brazos River further upstream. This suspension bridge, which served as a model for the Brooklyn Bridge, now carries pedestrians over the river (between the Washington and Franklin Avenue bridges, along North University Parks Boulevard).

What may be amusing to visitors is that Waco, the hometown of the Baptist-founded Baylor University, also once held Texas' largest regulated red light district. "Two Street," as it was called, is now home to the Convention Center and several restaurants along 2nd Avenue, which runs parallel to the Brazos River.

Be sure to stop by the famous Dr Pepper Museum, as Waco is the birthplace of Texas' favorite soft drink (300 5th Street). Baylor University displays lots of history – including a giant mammoth skeleton - inside the Mayborn Museum Complex (1300 South University Parks on the Baylor University Campus). Waco's past can be seen easily across the river on Elm Street, where the once bustling commercial district of a predominantly black neighborhood is now derelict and forgotten (Washington Avenue bridge, Washington Avenue turns into Elm Street).[28] For the kids, Waco is also home to Cameron Park Zoo (Herring Avenue).

Texas' first law enforcement /vigilante agency is honored in the Texas Rangers Hall of Fame and Museum with displays of weaponry dating back to the beginning of the Rangers and exhibits on some of the most notorious cases the Rangers cracked (at Interstate 35 and University Drive). The museum is located near the site of Fort Fisher, which the Texas Rangers established in 1837 to protect American settlers from hostile natives.

The Texas Rangers figured prominently in trail driving history. When barbed wire cut off the open range, the Rangers protected landowners from wire-cutting cowboys who wanted unrestricted access to watering holes.

Meridian
- Downtown
- Gas stations and restaurants

Directions:
1) From Washington Avenue in downtown Waco, turn north onto N. 4th Street (one way to the north).
2) Turn left (southwest) onto West Waco Drive/ US 84 and follow for approximately 2 miles.
3) Turn right (west)) onto Texas Loop 340/ TX 6.
4) Follow Loop 340/ TX 6 for approximately 44 miles to the intersection of TX 6 and TX 22.
5) Turn right (north) on TX 22 and follow it to downtown Meridian. TX 22 becomes Morgan Street in Meridian.

What's to See:
Meridian is the tiny county seat of Bosque County, a predominantly Norwegian region nestled in the northern Hill Country. This quiet village doesn't offer many sights for the Chisholm Trail hunter, though a branch of the trail did pass nearby – most likely along the path of the town's railroad tracks.

Kimball
- Ruins in a park

Directions:
1) From Morgan Street east of downtown Meridian, turn left (north) onto 7th Street/ TX 174.
2) Follow TX 174 for approximately 15 miles through Morgan to Kimball Bend Park (also called Chisholm Trail Park).
3) Turn left (north) into Kimball Bend Park and follow park roads.

What's to See:
Today Kimball is a tranquil area park with ruins that overlook the Brazos River. During the cattle drives, however, Kimball was anything but quiet. The normally placid Brazos could sometimes become a raging river, forcing the outfits to camp out and graze for extended periods of time. This made the trails all the more lucrative for entrepreneurs, who built Kimball as a supply stop, where businesses served the cowboys everything from horseshoes to coffee beans. The railroad bypassed Kimball, and the trails trickled to a halt after a more westerly route was chosen.

What makes the remnants of Kimball unique is that the town's buildings were made out of brick and stone, not wood. Many traces of the town remain because of the more sturdy construction material. Concerned local historians raised funds to erect fences around the old buildings in order to protect them from vandals. They are visible in the roadside park that hugs the Brazos River.

Cleburne
- Downtown, Layland Museum, and Chisholm Trail cut-outs
- Hotels, gas stations, and restaurants

Directions:
1) From Kimball Crossing Park, turn left (north) onto TX 174.
2) Continue on TX 174 for approximately 20 miles to Cleburne. TX 174 becomes Cleburne's Main Street.

What's to See:
Cleburne is a town built on transportation. It sits on the military road to Fort Graham, and grew to be the southwestern maintenance center for the Santa Fe Railroad. TX 174 – Cleburne's Main Street - approximates the feeder road for the Chisholm Trail. The Layland Museum, housed in the Carnegie Library in downtown Cleburne, holds informative displays and interesting photographs (210 N. Caddo Street). West of downtown is a fun park with re-created Chisholm Trail scenes, including cut-outs, a stagecoach, and a livery (Buddy Stewart Park on US 67).

Fort Worth
- Hell's Half Acre, Sundance Square, Stockyards Historic District, and Thistle Hill
- Hotels, gas stations, and restaurants

Directions:
1) From downtown Cleburne, follow Main Street/ TX 174 north for approximately 13 miles to the intersection of Northwest John Jones Road/ FM 731.
2) Turn left (north) onto Northwest John Jones Road/ FM 731 and follow it for approximately 10 miles to Altamesa Boulevard.
3) Turn right (east) onto Altamesa Boulevard.
4) Turn left (north) at the next intersection onto Village Parkway.

5) Continue north on Village Parkway for 6 miles. Village Parkway will become Hemphill Road north of the intersection with Edgecliff Road.
6) Turn right (east) onto West Rosedale Street.
7) Turn left (north) onto South Main Street/ US 287.
8) Follow South Main Street/ US 287 north into downtown Fort Worth.

What's to See:

    Texas' quintessential "cow town" got its start not along a trail, but as a military camp built to guard American settlers against hostile Native Americans. Camp Worth never even became a fort. Consisting of only canvass tents, this little settlement was governed by Fort Bird, a military stockade located in today's Birdville in northern Tarrant County.

Tenth Street was a busy place at the turn of the century.
Courtesy Fort Worth Public Library.

    The many feeder trails from the South began to congregate in Fort Worth after the Civil War, mainly because the Trinity River had easy-to-ford banks. The town also built livestock holding pens for buying, selling, and keeping cattle. Fort Worth quickly became *the* center for Texas livestock trading. When the railroad came to the town in the 1870s, forward thinking businessmen capitalized on Fort Worth's cow-friendly reputation and created the Stockyard Company just north of downtown. By the early 20th century, this brick-built warehouse district became home to hundreds of holding pens, the Swift and Armor meat packing plants, and the Stockyard's Board of Trade –some historians have called the Fort Worth stockyards "the Wall Street of the West."

Fort Worth's vice district was legendary. Hell's Half Acre, as the area around today's Lancaster Avenue and Houston Street was called, brimmed with bordellos, gambling parlors, saloons, and other dubious entertainment. While cowboys came to the district looking for a good time, they were often shafted by professional gamblers and assorted crooks, which appalled the local citizenry. After all, cowboys who've been fleeced could not spend their money in legitimate businesses. By 1900, Fort Worth had cleaned up Hell's Half Acre, but the area continued as a rather seedy outpost until the 1960s, when all of the buildings were razed to make way for the Water Gardens and Convention Center (South Main Street, Lancaster Avenue and South Houston Street).

Sundance Square, where Sam Bass supposedly hid out and Butch Cassidy partied with the Sundance Kid, is now an exciting entertainment district, with the Bass Performance Hall anchoring stores, restaurants, and night clubs (South Main Street and West 5th Street).

The Stockyards of Fort Worth were anchored by the Swift and Armour packing plants. Courtesy Fort Worth Public Library.

The crown jewel of Fort Worth's western past is the Stockyards National Historic District (North Main Street and Exchange Avenue). This "Wall Street of the West" is still an active futures exchange, though transactions are handled electronically instead of locally. Stores, restaurants, bars, and museums are housed in converted stock pens, while many of the old pens remain in their original condition. The world's most famous honky tonk, Billy Bob's, sits directly north of the Stockyards. The Grapevine Vintage Railroad ferries tourists through the stockyards and into downtown Fort Worth. Taking this train provides an excellent vantage point of vintage Fort Worth, as it crosses the Trinity River, where the cattle would bed for the night. You may see some cattle herds grazing there now.

The famous White Elephant Saloon welcomes everyone with its authentic wooden bar (106 East Exchange Avenue). The Star Café (109 West Exchange Avenue) is home to Miss Molly's Bed and Breakfast, which used to be a bordello. Two daily longhorn cattle drives enchant visitors, and a nightly rodeo brings yet another western feel to the district. For those visitors who want more authentic experiences, check out the towering ruins of the old Swift Processing Plant, at the end of Exchange Avenue east of the stockyards.

Weatherford Street housed saloons and brothels.
Courtesy Fort Worth Public Library.

Only a handful of cattle baron mansions from the early 20th century remain in Fort Worth. One of them, Thistle Hill was once home to Electra Waggoner - Wharton of the legendary ranching family. It is now a museum (1509 Pennsylvania Avenue).

Fort Worth is interesting not just for its history. As you drive north from Fort Worth along US 287, which approximates route of the main feeder trail into Oklahoma, you will notice how much the vegetation thins. Wide, drier prairies with small clusters of trees dominate the area known as the Cross Timbers region. The limestone escarpments become more visible, dried up creek beds cross the landscape, and the sky becomes a lot bigger. Further north, you'll be following the famous 98th Meridian – the point in the West where rainfall falls off dramatically.[29] The West now really begins.

Decatur
- Downtown, Wise County Museum, and Waggoner Mansion
- Hotels, gas stations, and restaurants

Directions:
1) Follow Main Street/ US 287 north out of downtown Fort Worth and the stockyards.
2) After approximately 19 miles, US 287 will merge with US 81 in Avondale. Continue following US 287/ US 81 north for approximately 23 miles to Decatur.
7) In Decatur, veer right South Business US 287/ US 81 and follow the road north into downtown Decatur. The road will bend sharply to the left (west) and becomes Walnut Street in downtown Decatur.

What's to See:
Your route on US 287 approximates the main feeder trail north of Fort Worth. Most of the towns on this road got their start from the railroads, though a few older pioneer settlements (like Blue Mound, which you will pass as you travel through Denton County) date from the antebellum period.

Many people have heard of the city's nickname, "Eighter from Decatur," which is a dice role that produces 2 fours. Legend has it that this role apparently won a game for (and spared the life of) a gambler.

Downtown Decatur boasts several beautiful buildings facing each other on a series of hills. One of these is "El Castile," an imposing Italianate mansion that was once home to the Waggoner clan (East Main Street).[30] The Wise County Museum overlooks the town on top of a hill from inside the former administration building of the Baptist College (1602 S. Trinity

Street). Downtown Decatur harks back to western days, with weathered wooden facades and an imposing courthouse edifice. A Chisholm Trail marker graces the courthouse lawn.

The fabulous "El Castile" in Decatur greets visitors from atop a hill. Photo by author.

Bowie
- Downtown and Chisholm Trail cutouts
- Gas stations and restaurants

Directions:
1) From downtown Decatur, take Walnut Street west to the intersection of US 81/ US 287.
2) Turn right (north) to merge onto US 81/ US 287
3) Follow US 81/ US 287 north for approximately 30 miles to Bowie.
3) In Bowie, US 81 and US 287 split. Make sure to follow US 81 north, which will lead you right into town. US 81 becomes Wise Street in Bowie.

What's to See:

On the trip from Decatur to Bowie, you'll pass through several small towns that sound like they were named by Western dime novelists. Alvord, one of these towns, was once surrounded by the petrified remains of a forest. Randalph B. Marcy mentioned these "crystallized cottonwoods" in his journal as he explored the Red River valley in 1856, and several homes and businesses in the area used the fossils for construction. Another colorfully named community, Sunset, welcomed the Butterfield Overland Stage Coach, which ceased running at the advent of the Civil War.

While Bowie owes its existence to the building of the railroad in the 1880s, settlers had already made their homes around the town before the Civil War. Bowie has a compact downtown and a nice Chisholm Trail roadside park on Wise Street, with comical cutouts and a replica of the historical marker that is located on private land at Red River Station further north.

Montague and Nocona
- Western heritage
- Gas stations and restaurants

Directions:
1) From Wise Street in downtown Bowie, follow Mason Street / TX 59 north for approximately 11 miles to Montague.
2) From Montague, follow FM 175 north for approximately 9 miles to US 82 in Nocona.

What's to See:

Along this route, you will follow one of the main feeder trails leading to Indian Territory, crossing straight through Montague County. Along this road, you will intersect with two other old trails: the 1849 California Road, which beckoned fortune seekers to find gold in California, and the Butterfield Overland Stage Coach Route. Montague County isn't called the "trail crossing county" for nothing!

While one wouldn't be able to tell by its size, little Montague serves as the county seat for Montague County. Established in the 1850s, the town experienced a brief boom brought on by rail traffic, but when the trains stopped coming, the town stopped growing.

Nocona is not a trail town, but got its start on the trail nonetheless: it usurped Spanish Fort, an original Chisholm Trail stop along the Red River, when the railroad chose a more southerly route. The famous boot maker H.J. Justin moved his shop to Nocona from Spanish Fort as well, cementing Nocona's reputation as an old-West outpost. The Tales 'n Trails Museum, which features exhibits on local history, can be found at 1522 East US 82.

Spanish Fort

- Centennial Markers, abandoned store, abandoned school, and cemetery

Directions:
1) From downtown US 82 in downtown Nocona, turn north onto Clay Street/ FM 103 and follow it for approximately 20 miles to Spanish Fort.

What's to See:

This little town, sitting almost forgotten at the every edge of Montague County, holds some of the most fascinating history in Texas. During the 18th century, a large French-Indian trading post occupied the site, centering a Taovayan (a subgroup of the Wichitas) settlement. The Comanches, who were both trading partners and allies with the Taoayans, set up winter camps alongside the post, creating a city of several thousand people.

In 1756, a war party comprised of Taovayan and Comanche men from the Red River trading post raided the Spanish mission at San Saba in Menard County. Although the mission was over 250 miles from the trading post, it was the closest Spanish settlement where the warriors could raid for horses, ammunition, and other items.[31] After they set the fort ablaze, killing several friars, the Spanish territorial government sent Captain Diego Ortiz Parilla and his men to capture the marauders and bring them to justice.

This store is the only remaining structure of downtown Spanish Fort. Photo by author.

Parilla and his troops trailed the warriors through mostly unknown territory. While all of Texas was under Spanish rule, northern Texas, with impressions of the "fierce" Comanches, the "tattooed" Wichitas, and the "cruel" Caddos, comprised a seemingly hostile area that most Spaniards were not willing to cross. When Parilla encountered unknown people along his pursuit, he burned their villages. However, Spanish-speaking natives helped him by showing him the possible route of the Comanches and Toavayans. The Spanish troops could not match the warriors in speed. Most were on foot, having to lug provisions and even a cannon.

Parilla's troops traced the raiding party all the way to the massive settlement along the Red River. Parilla quickly realized he was outnumbered, and after a brief shoot out, his regiment hightailed it back south. In their confusion, they left the cannon behind, which the Indian villagers promptly confiscated.[32]

Years later, the Taovayans, decimated by smallpox and other problems, abandoned the post and merged with the Comanches further west. They left behind an impressive if decaying fort and the captured Spanish cannon. American settlers became convinced the post was Spanish in origin. Hence Burlington, the original name for the new American settlement at the site, was renamed Spanish Fort.

Sitting just east of the main Chisholm Trail Red River crossing, and just south of federally regulated Indian Territory, Spanish Fort was a true frontier town. Gambling halls, saloons, hotels, a doctor's office, a supply store, an inspection station, and even a brothel hugged its muddy Main Street. H.J. Justin, a cobbler from Indiana, set up his first boot store in Spanish Fort to cash in on the many cowboys who needed good footwear. Like most towns in the Wild West, Spanish Fort had both distinguished citizens and transients up to no good – card sharps, outlaws, and assorted seedy folk preferred being there because, if trouble brewed, they could quickly slink over to Indian Territory, where Texas law could not touch them. One account mentions that on one Christmas morning, four men were shot and killed in the saloon.

Spanish Fort dwindled when the railroad bypassed it. After a short rebound during an oil field discovery in 1920s, Spanish Fort lost its post office and school, and today this little town with the exciting history is a ghost town.

A brick store dating to Spanish Fort's frontier days is the only building remaining on what used to be Main Street. The store sits across the 1936 Centennial Marker and park which commemorate the 1756 Spanish expedition. The old cemetery, just south of the store on FM 103, has hand carved tombstones.

Nearby Illinois Bend, east of Spanish Fort on FM 103, was also a crossing point for cattle drives. That crossing site is now the Taovaya Bridge over the Red River.

Red River Station
- Original river crossing, historical markers, and ruins

Directions:
1) From Spanish Fort, follow FM 103 south towards Nocona.
2) Turn right (west) onto FM 2849.
3) FM 2849 will make a left (southward) turn and become Gary Lane. Continue south on Gary Lane (unpaved).
3) Turn right (west) onto Red River Station Road (unpaved).
4) At one point, you will cross a cattle guard. For you non-Westerners, a cattle guard is a "gate in the sand" that marks when a road enters private property. Steel pipes, set into the ground in the road, do not allow cattle to venture outside of the property. You are free to drive on this road, and the guard will not harm your tires.
5) Continue on Red River Station Road until you come across a granite historical marker.

What's to See:

Red River Station, which consisted of a small general store and a few residences, marked an ancient buffalo crossing which also served the longhorns on the trail. Even if the river was more shallow and narrow along this crossing, that did not mean fording it was without peril. High water could strand the outfit for weeks, and the cattle got easily spooked along the soft sandy bottoms. Panicked cattle at the Red River crossing often left at least one cowboy dead.

Today, Red River Station's role in the cattle drives is commemorated by a granite marker, which reads:

"Jumping-off point" on the famous Chisholm Cattle Trail, (1867-87), Red River Station was a main crossing and last place on trail to buy supplies until Abilene, Kan.--350 miles north. During the cattle drive era of Western history, millions of animals swam the turbulent river here en route to Kansas railhead and markets. An abrupt bend in the river checked its flow at this point, creating a natural crossing which had been used for years by buffalo and Indians. Even so, the water was wide, swift, and sometimes clogged with sand bars. Frequently cattle were so jammed cowboys could walk across on their backs. Besides a cattle crossing, the station was an outpost of the frontier regiment, which patrolled Texas' northernmost border during Confederacy (1861-65). During cattle era, a town began here, its ferry serving drovers, soldiers, freighters, and settlers returning from Indian captivity. Local cemetery (1 mi. SE) contains many graves of these Texas pioneers."

In later years, a toll bridge marked Red River Station's river crossing, though the bridge is now long gone. A Boy Scout troop tried to mark the cow path from the historical marker to the actual crossing, and remnants of their efforts can still be seen. Further east on Red River Station Road is the cemetery, and a few remaining brick foundations betray that commerce once thrived here.

End of Chisholm Trail in Texas
Directions:
1) From Red River Station Road, backtrack to Nocona by taking Red River Station Road east to Gray Road, Gray Road north to FM 2849, and FM 2849 east to FM 103.
2) Follow FM 103 south to Nocona.
3) Turn right (west) onto US 82.

4) Follow US 82 for approximately 14 miles to the intersection of US 81 in Ringgold.
5) Follow the signs for US 81 north to Terral, Oklahoma.
6) Follow US 81 into Oklahoma, where you will continue your adventure up the Chisholm Trail.

Texas Chisholm Trail Tour 2 (1 day)
Fort Worth, Roanoke, Old Elizabethtown, Denton, Bolivar, Gainesville, Sivell's Bend, St. Jo, Nocona, and Ringgold

In Texas, many unnamed cattle trails converged north of Fort Worth to follow the Chisholm Trail. One of these secondary trails of the Texas Chisholm Trail took a more easterly course, going through Denton and Cooke counties.

Fort Worth
Your journey will begin at the Stockyards in Fort Worth on North Main Street and Exchange Avenue (see Texas Chisholm Trail Tour 1 for tourist information).

Roanoke
- Town Center
- Gas stations and restaurants

Directions:
1) Follow North Main Street/ US 287 north from the Fort Worth Stockyards to NE 28th Street.
2) Turn right (east) onto NE 28th Street/ TX 183.
5) Follow NE 28th Street/ TX 183 east to Belknap Street/ US 377.
6) Veer left (northeast) onto Belknap Street/ US 377.
7) After approximately 2 miles, veer left (north) to follow US 377/ Old Denton Highway.
8) Follow US 377/ Old Denton Highway for 14 miles into Roanoke.
9) Turn right (north) onto South Oak Street to get to downtown Roanoke.

What's to See:
Roanoke is the modern name of a series of much smaller settlements that date back to the late 1840s, when pioneers settled

around a fresh water source. From a humble well, the settlement grew into a well-known watering hole, where cattle drives passed through during the 1870s. Roanoke became a real town once the Texas and Pacific Railroad laid tracks nearby in the 1880s. A testament to Roanoke's heady growth is the restored Rock Building, a saloon and brothel built in 1886, which still stands at 114 North Oak Street.

Old Elizabethtown
- Cemetery

Directions:
1) From downtown Roanoke, return to US 377 and head north.
2) Turn left (northwest) onto Byron Nelson Boulevard / TX 114.
3) Turn left (west) onto Litsey Road.
4) Follow Litsey Road for approximately 2.5 miles to Elizabethtown Cemetery Road.
5) Turn right (north) onto Elizabethtown Cemetery Road and follow this road until you reach the cemetery.

What's to See:
   Though only the cemetery remains of Elizabethtown, this settlement was once a prominent supply stop for early cattle drives. The town vanished after citizens moved to nearby railroad towns like Justin and Roanoke.

Denton
- Pilot Knob, downtown, and Courthouse Museum
- Hotels, gas stations, and restaurants

Directions:
1) From the cemetery, turn right (north) onto Elizabethtown Cemetery Road and follow it north for approximately one mile.
2) Veer right (northeast) onto the feeder road for Interstate 35 W.
3) Merge onto Interstate 35 W.
4) Follow Interstate 35 W north for approximately 17 miles to Denton.
5) In Denton, Interstate 35 W merges with Interstate 35 E. Continue to follow Interstate 35 to the north towards Oklahoma.
8) Take Exit 469 = University Drive/ US 380, then turn right (east) onto University Drive/ US 380.

6) Follow University Drive/ US 380 east for approximately 4 miles, then turn right (south) onto Elm Street.
7) Elm Street will bring you into downtown Denton.
What's to See:

Cattle drivers described Denton as a dangerous and wild place, where Indian raids and brush fires were common. Today, Denton is quite cosmopolitan, home to both the University of North Texas and Texas Woman's University.

As you drive north on Interstate 35 W, you will encounter one of Denton's more noticeable landmarks. Pilot Knob, a large hill on the western side of Interstate 35 W just south of town, was supposedly used by settlers to warn of raiding Indians. Sam Bass, who worked at a local hotel and raced horses through the streets of Denton, is said to have hid out in a cave on the hill.

Denton County, organized in 1846, became a trading center known for its many pottery kilns. Two important universities have made Denton the cultural capital of the North Texas region. The University of North Texas, founded in 1890, is famous for its music program, and the picturesque Texas Woman's University campus holds the Little Chapel in the Woods, built by the Works Progress Administration in the 1930s and dedicated by Eleanor Roosevelt. The Denton County Courthouse Museum, situated inside the beautifully restored 1896 courthouse, tells of the county's history through photographs and artifact exhibits (downtown Denton square).

A branch of the Chisholm Trail ran just west of the town. Today, the Burlington Northern and Santa Fe Railroad parallel the old path. For almost a year, Denton was a stop for the Butterfield Overland Stagecoach until the company stopped driving through confederate Texas.

Bolivar
- Home to John S. Chisum

Directions:
1) From downtown Denton, go north on Locust Street/ US 77 (parallel to Elm Street on the east side of the courthouse) to University Boulevard/ US 380.
2) Turn left (west) onto University Boulevard / US 380 and follow it for approximately 2 miles to Interstate 35.

3) Turn right (north) onto the service road for Interstate 35.
4) Merge onto Interstate 35 and follow it north for approximately 12 miles to Sanger.
5) In Sanger, take Exit 478 = FM 455/ Slidell/ Bolivar and turn left (west) onto FM 455.
6) Follow FM 455 for approximately 7 miles to Bolivar.
What's to See:

    Though there's not much to see in modern Bolivar, it has a historical past. The Chisholm Trail passed just east of the town. Famous cattleman John S. Chisum, known for marking his cattle by slicing their ears, owned a ranch in Bolivar prior to establishing his better-known digs in Roswell, New Mexico. A 1936 Texas Centennial Historical Marker commemorates the site of his former ranch house.

    John S. Chisum was an interesting man. He valued privacy above all other things, probably because he had allegedly created a family with his slave concubine and did not want anyone to interfere. Although regional lore maintains that he left Texas for New Mexico to escape the encroachment of farmers, he may have left Texas because of its miscegenation laws.

Gainesville

- Downtown, Santa Fe Depot, hanging tree, and Morton Museum
- Hotels, gas stations, restaurants

Directions:
1) From Bolivar, continue to follow FM 455 west, past Slidell, to the intersection of FM 455 and FM 51.
2) Turn right (northeast) onto FM 51 and follow it for approximately 24 miles north to Gainesville. FM 51 becomes California Street in Gainesville.
3) Follow California Street to downtown Gainesville.
What's to See:

    Gainesville, a supply stop for cowboys on the trail, was once quite a rough frontier town. With its proximity to Indian Territory, many a shady character wandered its streets – moonshiners, slave traders, gamblers, and swindlers who could leave Texas quickly whenever they felt trouble brewed. For decades after the trail drives ended, the thick brush country just north of the Red River was considered a bandit's roost.

Prior to Reconstruction, Gainesville was also one of the western-most towns in Texas, and raids by the hostile Comanches and Kiowas were not uncommon before and during the Civil War. Confederates and Unionists clashed violently in Gainesville, where Unionists – called "Jayhawkers" – were hung for their resistance to the draft. The hanging tree still stands in Pecan Creek Park (take Lindsay Street south from California Street, east of downtown). More local history is available at the Morton Museum, located inside a restored firehouse (210 South Dixon Street).

The main thoroughfare in Gainesville, California Street, was named for the gold-rush trail forged by Randalph B. Marcy in the 1850s.

Sivell's Bend
- P.O.W Camp and Chisholm Trail crossing

Directions:
1) From downtown Gainesville, take California Street west to Interstate 35.
2) Turn north onto Interstate 35 for one mile (you must enter Interstate 35 – the feeder road will dead end).
3) Take Exit 498 B = US 82 West/ Wichita Falls.
4) Merge onto US 82 and follow it west for approximately 2 miles to FM 1201.
4) Turn right (north) onto FM 1201.
5) Follow FM 1201 north for approximately 15 miles to Sivell's Bend.

What's to See:
Along FM 1201, you will see many ruins, consisting of chimneys, concrete piers, and shells of houses: these are the remnants of a WWII prisoner of war camp, which used to house German prisoners.

At the end of FM 1201 you will find the community of Sivell's Bend, which used to supply drovers on the Chisholm Trail before they crossed the Red River here. Today, only a small school, some houses, and a cemetery remain of the town. A ferry also crossed the Red River at Sivell's Bend. The actual crossing site is now on private land – FM 1201 dead-ends into a private driveway.

St. Jo
- Head of Elm Cemetery and Stonewall Saloon
- Gas stations

Directions:
1) From Sivell's Bend, backtrack on FM 1201 to US 82.
2) Turn right (west) onto US 82.
3) Follow US 82 west for approximately 21 miles to St. Jo.

What's to See:
St. Jo is a small town today, but was once a very busy trail intersection. Early settlers called St. Jo "Head of Elm" because the original town site was situated above the headwaters of the Elm Fork of the Trinity River. It was due to this location that the gold rush trail, the Butterfield Overland Stage Coach, the U.S. Army's military road, and a branch of the Texas Chisholm Trail converged on this town. The Stonewall Saloon (closed as of this writing), an original Chisholm Trail relic, still stands on the northwest corner of the square.

The Stonewall Saloon in St. Jo harks back to frontier days. Photo by author.

End of Chisholm Trail in Texas
Directions:
1) From St. Jo, follow US 82 west for approximately 26 miles to Ringgold. You will pass Nocona (and from Nocona, Spanish Fort

and Red River Station,) on your way, so you can visit the locations on Tour 1 to make this leg of your trip through Texas complete.
2) In Ringgold, follow signs to US 81.
3) Take US 81 north to Oklahoma.

Indian Territory a.k.a. Oklahoma Chisholm Trail Tour (2 days)
Fleetwood, Ryan, Waurika, Addington, Duncan, Marlow, Rush Springs, Chickasha, El Reno, Geary, Kingfisher, Dover, Hennessey, Red Fork Station, Enid Kremlin, Pond Creek, Jefferson and Medford

The landscape of Oklahoma along the Chisholm Trail differs greatly from that along the Shawnee Trail: fewer trees, flatter vistas, and drier air. You are now in the southern plains, where the buffalo once roamed. In Oklahoma, you'll enter the Cross Timbers Region, with its dense stands of trees that lie between vast open spaces with small streams that crisscross the landscape. Many of the small waterways in the area were named by the cowboys who may have been recalling a sight or an experience: Cow Creek, Bear Crossing Creek, Snake Creek, and Wildhorse Creek, to name a few.

For the most part, the Chisholm Trail sites in Oklahoma are not contemporaries of the trail. In the south, the trail skirted the western edge of the Chickasaw Nation, then entered unassigned lands in the central part of the territory.[33] Crossing the Cherokee Outlet on its way to Kansas, the cattle drivers did not pass many towns, but rather little trading posts that served the cowboys as well as the Plains Indians.

Most drives in Indian Territory were uneventful, simply because the drivers did not meet many people. Weather more than made up for the lack of human interaction. The Chisholm Trail lies directly in "Tornado Alley," and trail drivers recalled the strong storms, howling winds, blizzards, flash floods, and twisters that bore down on them.

As you drive along US 81, you will parallel two important lines: the Chisholm Trail about a mile to the east, and the 98th Meridian – the line "where the West begins" - a mile to the west.

From any of these little towns, take a main road to the east and you will find a cement post commemorating the actual Chisholm Trail. Go west, and you will come across a dirt road marked with a "US 98th Meridian" street sign, which designates the western boundary of the Chickasaw Nation and the historic dividing line between Indian and Oklahoma Territories.

Fleetwood
- Old Store and Chisholm Trial Markers
- Gas station and restaurant

Directions:
1) Follow US 81 north to Terral, Oklahoma.
2) In Terral, turn right (east) onto Main Street.
3) Follow Main Street for approximately 4-5 miles. Fleetwood – which comprises an abandoned store - will be on your left.

What's to See:
Just east of Terral, you'll come upon the actual trail and the old trading post town of Fleetwood.

The old store at Fleetwood sits just west of the Chisholm Trail. Photo by author.

While it takes a good twenty minutes to drive from Red River Station, Texas, to Fleetwood, Oklahoma, they are actually only about three miles apart as the crow flies (or as the cow roams). Fleetwood was the only place in southern Indian Territory in the early days of the Chisholm Trail where cattle drivers could obtain supplies. The actual trail is marked a half mile east of the Fleetwood historical marker.

An abandoned brick store occupies the site of the old trading post. Behind it lie the ruins of the Fleetwood school. The Chisholm Trail marker is on a small hill, providing a good vantage point to see depressions in the ground that the cattle on the trail made.

Ryan
- Mural and Roadside Park
- Gas stations, restaurants

Directions:
1) From the Fleetwood Store, backtrack to Terral.
2) Turn right (north) onto US 81.
3) Follow US 81 north for approximately 9 miles to Ryan.

What's to See:
A tidy town with a bricked main street, Ryan has a billboard with a mural of the Chisholm Trail located on the side of downtown building (NW corner of US 81). A roadside park on OK 32 (east) celebrates the trail.

Waurika
- Chisholm Trail Museum and Rock Island Depot
- Gas stations, restaurants

Directions:
1) From Ryan, follow US 81 north for approximately 10 miles to the intersection of US 81/ US 70 in Waurika.
2) Turn left (west) onto US 70 and follow it for 1 mile to the town center of Waurika. Turn right (east) onto US 70 and follow it for approximately a quarter mile to visit the Chisholm Trail Museum.

What's to See:
Waurika is a railroad and farming town, small and unassuming, but with a rather large Rock Island train station in the center of town.

The town is rightfully proud of its Chisholm Trail heritage, which is displayed in a very interesting museum (US 70 just east of US 81). One of the ladies who runs the museum is a descendent of Black Beaver, an original Chisholm Trail blazer. The exhibits are great, and pay homage to the Plains Indians as well as the drovers.

Note that the museum may only be open sporadically as it is run by volunteers.

Addington
- Monument Hill

Directions:
1) From Waurika, follow US 81 north for approximately 6 miles to Addington.
2) In Addington, turn right (east) onto Eva Road/E 1910/ Monument Road. This road is the northern-most road within the township of Addington.
3) Follow Eva Road/ E 1910/ Monument Road east to the monument – you can't miss it, as it sits on the highest hill in Jefferson County.

What's to See:
Addington lies just west of one of the tallest vistas on the trail. Founded by the railroad in the 1890s, Addington succumbed to bank robberies and the Great Depression. With its downtown boarded up and falling in, Addington, with a dwindling population, is now a ghost town.

African American cowboy Tom Lattimore, who took several trips up the Chisholm Trail, is buried on top of Monument Hill. Photo by author.

Jefferson County commemorates the Chisholm Trail with a granite marker at the top of Monument Hill. The sweeping views will take your breath away. This hill served as a camp ground, look out point, and as an identifiable mark on the trail. Trail graffiti has been found etched in rock (on private land), and the grave of trail driver Tom Latimore is located on the southeastern corner of the site. East of the hill is another white marker, denoting the actual trail. Looking west towards Monument Hill from the white marker, you can easily identify the depressions made by the cattle's hooves so many years ago.

Duncan
- Chisholm Trail Heritage Center and Parks
- Hotels, gas stations, and restaurants

Directions:
1) From Monument Hill in Addington, backtrack to US 81. Turn right (north) onto US 81 and follow it for approximately 19 miles to Duncan.

What's to See:
Duncan is a lovely town, with clean broad streets and lots of recreational opportunities. It is also very kid-friendly, with many playgrounds around town – after all, this is where Opie Taylor/Richie Cunningham (a.k.a. Ron Howard) was born. The city has a handsome downtown and commemorates the Chisholm Trail with a festival every May. The trail ran through downtown Duncan.

The Chisholm Trail Heritage Center (1000 Chisholm Trail Parkway) is a state-of-the-art museum with interactive displays, an animatronic Jesse Chisholm, a 4-D theater, and a world-class statue of a trail drive. The museum is especially geared towards children and is worth an extensive visit.

Marlow
- Trail history
- Gas stations and restaurants

Directions:
1) From Duncan, continue north on US 81 for 10 miles to Marlow.

What's to See:
Marlow's first residents were people who did business with the Chisholm Trail drivers, either as suppliers or as customers for the longhorns (some of Marlow's more enterprising souls would purposely stampede the herds to make money off of "strays" they would just happen to come across). Founded in the 1880s, Marlow's trail days succumbed when the Rock Island railroad laid

tracks directly on the trail. The tracks parallel US 81 all the way to Kansas.

Rush Springs
- Trail history
- Gas stations and restaurants

Directions:
1) From Marlow, continue north on US 81 for 10 miles to Rush Springs.

What's to See:
    While most towns in Oklahoma have tenuous ties to the Chisholm Trail at best, Rush Springs is the real deal. As its name suggests, the town is home to natural springs, making the area an ideal watering stop for thirsty cattle. With its fortunate location, Rush Springs became an intersecting point for many trails, such as the military road that helped to supply Fort Sill and a stage coach line that connected to the Choctaw Nation in the east.

    Due to the springs on the arid plains, Rush Springs seemed to have been inhabited by many different people over centuries, if not millennia. In the 1850s, a Wichita tribe settled along the springs, but they fled to Fort Arbuckle in the Chickasaw Nation after the Battle of Wichita Village (1858) between the Comanches and the U.S. army.

    Rush Springs claims to be the Watermelon Capital of Oklahoma, if not the United States, and who's going to argue with that?

Chickasha
- Railroad history
- Hotels, gas stations and restaurants

Directions:
1) From Rush Springs, continue on US 81 north for approximately 18 miles to downtown Chickasha.
2) In Chickasha, US 81 will merge with US 277 to become South 4th Street/ US 81 / US 277.

What's to See:
    Chickasha is a rather large town with a busy city center. The railroad is still very active here. The town, which is the seat to the Kiowa Nation, does not offer much in the way of Chisholm Trail

history. The trail passed east of the town site along the Chicago, Rock Island, and Pacific Railroad tracks, which were laid in the 1890s.

El Reno
- Downtown (Route 66), Fort Reno, and Canadian County Historical Museum
- Hotels, gas stations, and restaurants

Directions:
1) From downtown Chickasha, follow South 4th Street / US 81 / US 277 north to Choctaw Avenue / US 81 / US 62.
2) Turn left (west) onto Choctaw Avenue / US 81 / US 62.
3) Turn right (north) onto US 81.
4) Continue north on US 81 for approximately 32 miles to El Reno.
5) To get to downtown El Reno, turn left (west) onto SE 27th Street/ OK 66.
6) Take an immediate right (north) onto Rock Island Avenue / US 81/ OK 66 and follow it north into town.

What's to See:

El Reno makes the most out of being at the crossroads of two famous roads – the Chisholm Trail and Route 66. The town is an offshoot of a frontier fort, which served to protect an Indian agency outpost. Today, the town is very conscious of its importance in Oklahoma's history. As it also sits on a major interstate, El Reno is a very busy place with many restaurants, hotels, and attractions.

In downtown El Reno, Rock Island Avenue and Main Street are vintage Route 66 roads, with Main Street being an older alignment. You can tour the town with tourist trolleys that recreate the era when street cars were prominent on El Reno streets. The Canadian County Historical Museum (300 South Grand), housed inside the restored Rock Island depot, sits on the 98th Meridian, which divided Indian and Oklahoma territory. Fort Reno (7101 West Cheyenne) recalls pioneers, the Chisholm Trail, and the Indian wars through reenactors, restored buildings, and faithful historic interpretations. One of the many purposes of the fort was as a "remount station," where cavalry exchanged horses and mules. "Buffalo Soldiers" and General Sheridan at one time called Fort Reno home.

Geary
- Jesse Chisholm's Grave at Left Hand Spring

Directions:
1) From Rock Island Avenue / US 81 in downtown El Reno, take Sunset Drive west.
2) Follow Sunset Drive for approximately 5 miles to Interstate 40.
3) Take Interstate 40 west.
4) Follow Interstate 40 west for approximately 10 miles. Take exit 108 = US 281 and follow US 281 north for approximately 8 miles to Geary.
5) In Geary, turn right (east) onto NW 2nd Street.
6) Turn left (northeast) onto County Line Road / N 2630. Follow this road for approximately 4 miles.
7) Turn right (east) onto 220th Street NE / E 0910 (unpaved).
8) Turn left (north) onto Chisholm Road / N 2650. This will be your second left (unpaved).
9) Turn left (west) onto 248th Street NW/ E 0890 and follow to the end of the road – there will be signs (unpaved).

Jesse Chisholm's grave at Left Hand Spring. Photo by author.

What's to See:

Geary, an old Route 66 town, is also the town nearest Jesse Chisholm's grave.

Chisholm became violently ill while camping along the creek and subsequently died. His friends buried him, marking his grave with whatever stones were available. As Geary developed years later, town folk knew that this famous man was buried somewhere in the vicinity, but without a decent marker, his grave proved hard to find. Geary elementary students took it upon themselves to collect all the pennies they could find, beg, and save and bought a simple but very moving tombstone for the old trail blazer. The inscription reads: "No one left his home cold or hungry."

Close to Chisholm's grave, in an unmarked location, lies Chief Left Hand of the Arapahos, who signed the Medicine Lodge Treaty and helped to found the Ghost Dance movement in Indian Territory.

Kingfisher
- Chisholm Trail Museum and Seay Mansion
- Gas stations and restaurants

Directions:
1) Backtrack from Jesse Chisholm's grave to Geary.
2) In Geary, turn left (east) onto US 270. This is old Route 66.
4) Follow US 270 east to Calumet.
5) In Calumet, US 270 jogs to the south. Continue on US 270 to the Interstate 40 intersection.
6) Take Interstate 40 east to El Reno.
7) In El Reno, take exit 119 = Business 40/ Sunset Drive/ Old Route 66 east towards downtown El Reno.
8) In downtown El Reno, turn left (north) onto North Choctaw Avenue / US 81.
9) Follow US 81 north for approximately 24 miles to Kingfisher. US 81 is Kingfisher's Main Street.

What's to See:

The first leg of this hour-long journey will take you along the original alignment of Route 66, which is always a fun drive. On US 81, you will drive over the North Canadian River. The trail drivers forded the river further upstream, where the Rock Island Railroad tracks cross it today. North on US 81, you will pass through Okarche, a predominantly German community that is home to Eischen's, "Oklahoma's Oldest Bar."

Residents call Kingfisher the "Buckle of the Wheat Belt," and they have a cool welcome sign to prove it. This is a pin-neat community with a wonderful Chisholm Trail Museum that chronicles not only Native American life and the Chisholm Trail, but Oklahoma pioneer and agricultural history as well (605 Zellers Avenue).

Kingfisher's museum lies directly on the Chisholm Trail. The museum is housed in an old nursing home, providing ample room for its many displays. In the back is an open air museum, which is a replica of an early 20th century town, complete with jail and pioneer cabins, one of which is said to have belonged to the mother of the Dalton boys. The Seay Mansion, home of the first governor of Oklahoma, lies just across the street and is available for touring.

Dover, Hennessey, and Red Fork Station
- Roadside Park
- Gas stations

Directions:
1) From US 81 in Kingfisher, head north for approximately 10 miles to Dover, then continue north on US 81 for 9 miles to Hennessey.

What's to See:
As you leave Kingfisher, you will begin traveling on the original surveyed portion of the Chisholm Trail. This road, blazed by Jesse Chisholm, at first served the military, natives, and pioneers before the cattle drives came through. Dover is the site of Red Fork Station, a supply point, market center, and stockade where locals bought and traded cattle. A roadside park commemorates the trail. The trail ran right along the park, and the imprint is slightly visible if you look really hard.

In the vicinity of Hennessey is the site of the brutal murder of wagon master Pat Hennessey and his men, George Fant, Thomas Calloway, and Ed Cook. The outfit, which bought supplies from the various ranches in the area and sold them to Indian agencies and Fort Sill, was ambushed and killed in 1874 by either a band of Osages and Cheyennes or by white rustlers, disguised as Cheyennes– the few eye witness accounts conflicted greatly.

Enid
- Railroad Museum of Oklahoma
- Hotels, gas stations and restaurants

Directions:
1) From Hennessey, continue north on US 81 to Enid. In Enid, US 81 becomes Van Buren Street.
What's to See:
Enid came into being in 1893 after a fevered land rush into the Cherokee Outlet, though the Chisholm Trail actually passed through what would become the center of town. Some town historians claim that Enid got its name from cattle drivers who turned a sign for "Dine" around. They could be joking, too. Many railroads intersected in Enid, making for an economic boom that is still going strong today. The Railroad Museum of Oklahoma in downtown Enid (702 N. Washington) can tell you more. Enid is also home to Northwestern Oklahoma State University.

About 30 minutes west of Enid on US 60 (take US 60 west to OK 8/ OK 45, go north on OK 8/OK 45) is the last remaining sod house in Oklahoma, complete with gift shop.

Kremlin and Cherokee Outlet
- Gas stations

1) From Enid, continue north on Van Buren Street / US 81 for approximately 15 miles. US 81 shares the road with US 60 and US 61.
2) Turn right (east) onto E 0320 to Kremlin.
What's to See:
This portion of the trip mirrors the land rushes of the Cherokee Outlet in the last quarter of the 19th century. The Cherokee Outlet had been leased by the Cherokees to a consortium of Texas cattlemen, who wanted to fatten their cattle on the luscious prairie grasses before selling them. This agreement worked well for the Cherokees, as it gave them a steady income and a use for the land. The federal government, however, believed the Cherokee Outlet did not belong to the Cherokees and forced the outlet to be opened for settlement to non-Cherokees, essentially ignoring several treaties and court decisions.

Kremlin's first inhabitants were Russians (how'd you guess?), but they were actually of German descent. Having settled in Russia around the Volga River at the behest of Catherine the Great, these Germans were forced to leave during a bout of Russian nationalism. They ended up settling in the plains of northern Oklahoma and southern Kansas, perhaps because the region looked similar to the Russian plains they had to leave behind.

The Chisholm Trail ran through the eastern side of town.

Pond Creek, Jefferson, Medford

1) Backtrack to US 81 from Kremlin, then continue north on US 81.
2) Turn right (east) onto US 81/ US 60 and follow it to Pond Creek.
3) In Pond Creek, make sure to keep north on US 81.
4) Follow US 81 to Medford.

Directions:
What's to See:

Pond Creek was a Chisholm Trail Crossing and stage coach stop before it became a town founded by land rush settlers.

A private fort once sat where Jefferson is now, which became a farming center when the railroads came through.

Medford is an unassuming town that thanks its existence to agriculture. A plaque on the courthouse lawn commemorates the Chisholm Trail. After Medford, you will drive straight into Kansas.

Kansas Chisholm Trail Tour (2 days)
Caldwell, Wellington, Wichita, Newton, Lehigh, and Abilene

Upon leaving Oklahoma, you'll notice a gradual upwelling of the landscape – contrary to popular assumption, Kansas is not so flat. At this point, US 81 is very isolated, and all the little communities in the area center around farms. Years ago, when cattle trailed through this very region, the landscape looked very different – it held fewer trees and consisted mainly of prairie grasses.

When exiting Indian Territory, the cowboys found themselves back on "American" (as opposed to Indian Nation). On the Kansas plains, the Chisholm Trail, which pioneers also called the Texas Trail, formed a wide path and a straight shot to Abilene. Though the trail was still far west of the "sod busters," central Kansas found itself in a settlement boom, and the trail drivers inadvertently fostered this development. Towns like Newton,

Caldwell, Abilene, and Ellsworth made reputations for themselves as places to obtain both good prices and good entertainment. These little Kansas outposts have become what we would consider the quintessential "cow towns," where shady characters tried to relieve cowboys of their money.

Once you enter Kansas, you'll find a roadside park commemorating the Chisholm Trail and the pioneers who settled here. Look for old wagon ruts, carved by pioneers, in the hills across the street. Beside the railroad tracks at the park is the famed Chisholm Trail panorama, consisting of life-sized cut-outs depicting a trail drive. They are situated directly on the Chisholm Trail.

You will follow US 81, then KS 15, for the last leg of your journey up the Chisholm Trail.

Upon entering Kansas, you'll be greeted by the shadow of a trail drive. Photo by author.

Caldwell
- Trail cutouts, downtown walking tour, and Boot Hill Cemetery
- Gas stations and restaurants

Directions:
1) From Medford, Oklahoma follow US 81 north for 17 miles to Caldwell.

What's to See:
Caldwell, called the "Border Queen," was the place for cattle drivers to live it up after crossing the relatively isolated Indian

Territory. The town has not changed much from its early days, except now it's much more respectable. Some of the frontier brick buildings are still in use. There's even a saloon downtown.

Today, Caldwell is a picturesque farming community, but with historically minded citizens: they established a downtown walking tour where they marked the locations of infamous gun battles and where notorious saloons and bawdy houses once entertained. To the north, Caldwell's Boot Hill Cemetery (pauper's graveyard) is small but well preserved.

Wellington
- Sumner County Museum
- Gas stations and restaurants

Directions:
1) From Caldwell, continue north on US 81 to the intersection of US 81/ W 175th Street.
2) Turn right (east) onto US 81/ W 175th Street and continue along this road to South Haven.
3) In South Haven, turn left (north) onto US 81/ South Hoover Road and continue north to Wellington (a 40 mile trip in all).

What's to See:
Wellington is a picturesque farming town that grew up around the Chisholm Trail, which passed just west of US 81. The Sumner County Museum, which holds Chisholm Trail displays, was once the county hospital (502 North Washington). On weekdays, you can check out the skull of a wooly mammoth at the courthouse. The Carnegie Library retains its original function.

Wichita
- Douglas Avenue, Cowtown Museum, Sedgwick County Museum, Kansas Aviation Museum and Old Town Market Place District
- Hotels, gas stations, and restaurants

Directions:
1) From Wellington, continue north on US 81. Note that in Wellington, US 81 jogs through town as North G Street and then 15th Street. Make sure to follow the signs.
2) Turn left (north) at the intersection of US 81/ North A Street.

3) Continue north on US 81. In Wichita, the signs for US 81 will also read Broadway.
4) Your starting point in Wichita is the intersection of Broadway/US 81 and Douglas Avenue (the actual trail through the city).
What's to See:
    Just southwest of Wichita lies Haysville, where cattle crossed Cowskin Creek (now a hiking and biking trail). Legend has it that a blizzard froze to death hundreds of cattle, and the drovers skinned them in order to recoup some of their investment – hence the name, Cowskin Creek.

    Wichita is a beautiful city and only second in size to Fort Worth along the Chisholm Trail. The city has eagerly embraced its cow town and railroad heritage.

Chisholm Trail monument on Douglas Avenue. Photo by author.

    Wichita began just after the civil war as a trading post, ferry, and cattle crossing where the Arkansas River and the Little Arkansas River met. Wichita prospered greatly from the Chisholm Trail, and drovers found respite in the Delano District, where brothels and saloons awaited them. After the cattle drives diminished, Wichita focused on agriculture and the air craft industry. By the mid-20th century, the city was also home to many drive-ins, motor courts, and original chain restaurants, with all their neon glory.[34]

    The Chisholm Trail meandered southwest of Wichita along the 98th Meridian (called Meridian Street in Wichita, west of downtown), then turned east to ford the rivers at Wichita. Therefore, the original Chisholm Trail can be followed along

Douglas Avenue, Wichita's main east-west thoroughfare. Along the west side of Douglas Avenue, road signs and statues mark the trail, culminating into an ornate granite marker in the center of the road.

The museums along Museum Boulevard are situated on the former grazing spots and river crossings, and are not far from the original site of Wichita's saloon district. Cowtown Museum offers a look at what Wichita was like during the trail days (1865 Museum Boulevard). Nearby is the Wichita Art Museum (1400 West Museum Boulevard).

The Sedgewick County Museum (204 South Main Street) is housed in Wichita's magnificent courthouse. Kansas' close ties to aeronautics are recounted at the Kansas Aviation Museum (3350 South George Washington Boulevard).

On East Douglas Avenue east of downtown lies the Old Town Market Place District, where manufacturing, industry, and commerce met the railroad among elevated platforms and red brick warehouses. Great restaurants, neighborhood pubs, fun museums, and authentic traces of Wichita's railroad and manufacturing past are present everywhere, including the Great Plains Transportation Museum (700 East Douglas; open seasonally on weekends). The Old Market Place is a vastly interesting area where you can explore Wichita history to your heart's content.

Further down Douglas Avenue is the absolutely gorgeous Wichita High School East, made of solid stone and built in the gothic style.

Newton
- Railroad depot, Kauffman Museum, and Harvey County Museum
- Gas stations and restaurants

Directions:
1) From downtown Wichita, take East Douglas Avenue east to US 81/ Interstate 135 / KS 15.
2) Go north on US 81/ Interstate 135 towards Newton.
3) In Newton, take Exit 30 = KS 15 to the northwest.
4) Turn right (north) onto Kansas Avenue/ KS 15.
5) Make sure to follow KS 15 as it jogs through town: it will become Washington Road, then Main Street.

What's to See:

Today Newton is a tidy town, but at one point it was called "the wickedest town in the West" after it became a cattle shipping center. The railroad is still very active, centering on an impressive depot that was built to resemble Shakespeare's house in Stratford-on-Avon. The Chamber of Commerce and law offices now share offices there.

Newton's handsome downtown is worth a stroll. The Kauffman Museum, which celebrates Newton's Native American, Mennonite, and pioneer heritage, sits directly on the Chisholm Trail (2701 North Main). The Harvey County Museum is housed in the well preserved Carnegie Library (203 North Main).

Lehigh
- Original Trail

Directions:
1) From Newton, motor north on Kansas Avenue / KS 15 for approximately 24 miles to the intersection of KS 15 and US 56 at Lehigh.

What's to See:
As you drive up this road, you will notice the distinctive old-world feel of the farms and communities around you. Goessel, a village located half-way between Newton and Lehigh, is a Mennonite community that practices many traditional ways. At the Alexanderwohl Mennonite Church, an impressive wooden structure, helpful signs convey the community's history. Further north, a marker at a roadside park explains the role of the Chisholm Trail, also known as the Texas Trail or Texas Road.

At Lehigh, the surveyed portion of the Chisholm Trail is plain to see. Photo by author.

Abilene
- Downtown, Union Pacific Terminus, Dwight D. Eisenhower Presidential Library, Old Town Abilene, Dickinson County Museum and Lebold Mansion
- Hotels, gas stations, and restaurants

Directions:
1) At the junction of KS 15 and US 56 in Lehigh, turn right (east) onto US 56/ KS 15.
2) Turn left (north) onto KS 15 and follow it north for approximately 45 miles to Abilene.
3) In Abilene, KS 15 becomes Broadway Avenue.

What's to See:

Yeehaw, pardner, we made it! Abilene is truly a delightful, handsome town that is very proud of its heritage: not only did the Chisholm Trail terminate here, but this is where Dwight D. Eisenhower grew up. A beautiful park has been landscaped around the retirement home of the former president, complete with meditation chapel and research library (200 SE 4th Street). Make sure to stroll through downtown Abilene. Local kids on their bikes and scooters, buying ice cream at the drugstore, hark back to safer, simpler times.

False façade at the Chisholm Trail terminus. Photo by author.

Abilene, a true town of the rails, boasts three train stations. The Union Pacific Station, now the Visitor's Center, is in front of the Chisholm Trail terminus (201 NW 2nd Street). This is where Joseph McCoy built stockades for the cattle to await shipment to

Kansas City. Take Texas Street (behind the Visitor's Center) and find the commemorative Chisholm Trail marker. Another depot, a rather simple brick structure, is located just south of the Visitor's Bureau.

Old Town Abilene, an outdoor museum, has many recreated buildings to see, such as the old school house, timber-cut cabins, jail house, and the beautiful Rock Island Depot from the 1880s (100 SE 5th Street). At the depot, catch a diesel train that takes passengers on an hour long journey through Kansas alfalfa fields and over the Smoky Hill River.

Near the Old Town museum complex is the Dickinson County Museum (412 South Campbell). Don't miss the Lebold Mansion, an ornate Italianate structure built upon the first dugout in Abilene (106 North Vine).

About an hour west of Abilene on Interstate 70 is Ellsworth. Ellsworth was founded as a direct competitor to the Abilene cattle shipment trade. Once the railroad came through, Ellsworth gave Abilene a real run for its money, even handing out posters to cattlemen to convince them to use the Ellsworth terminus instead.

End of the Chisholm Trail

Of all the cattle trails detailed in this guide, the Chisholm Trail proves to be not only the easiest, but also the most exciting to follow. Though its landscape isn't as scenic as that of the Great Western Trail, or its history quite as ancient as that of the Shawnee Trail, the Chisholm Trail is known the world over – for many people around the world, it epitomizes the West.

Chapter Four

FOLLOWING THE GREAT WESTERN TRAIL

Ruins of Fort Phantom Hill near Abilene, Texas. Photo by author.

Like most Texas drovers who went up the Chisholm Trail, John Lytle, a cattle ranger from Atascosa County, Texas thought the Chisholm Trail had become too crowded. Instead, Lytle's cattle drive outfit decided to follow an older feeder trail that ran through the fabled Texas Hill Country. They then continued to blaze a new trail that skirted the sacred Wichita Mountains in Indian Territory and followed along the mythical Big Basin in Kansas. This trail became known as the Great Western Trail, so-named to distinguish it from the Chisholm (or Eastern) Trail. By the 1880s, the Great Western Trail, which was called the Texas Cattle Trail in Oklahoma, became the preferred cattle road.[35] Cowboys also called it the Dodge City Trail or Fort Griffin Trail.

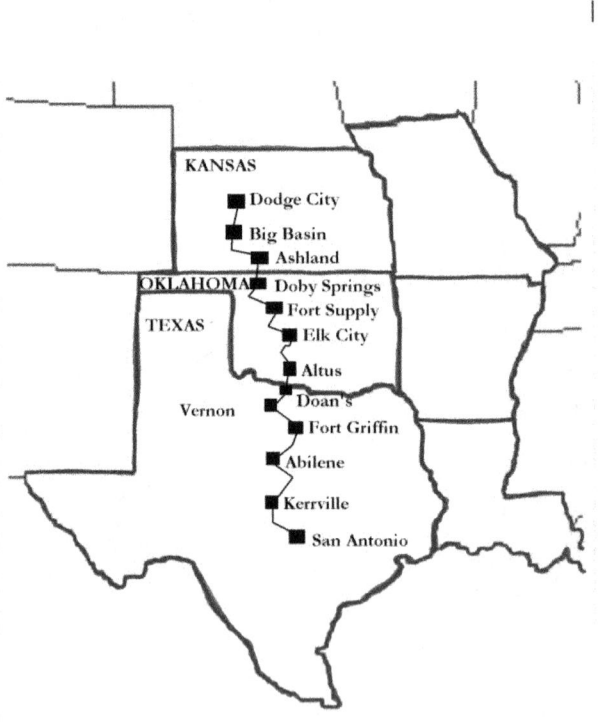

The Great Western Trail zig-zags across the Great Plains.

As with all trails, the Great Western Trail converged from feeder trails in Texas into a more cohesive road in Indian Territory. The tribes of the Southern Plains resented the white man's intrusions, especially the millions of cattle who scared the buffalo away and trampled over their meager land allotments. The hostility between the Texans and the Indians could be palatable at times, such as when trail driver F.M. Horton refused payment to Running Buffalo, a Cheyenne. Running Buffalo tried to stampede the herd and was shot by Horton. Horton, then, had to seek refuge from outraged Cheyenne warriors at Fort Supply just to escape with his life.[36]

Indian men often caused stampedes when their demand for tolls in the form of beef, or "wohaw," went unanswered.[37] But other members of the many tribes on the Plains adapted well to their situations. The Tonkawas, for example, saw cattle as a substitute for buffalo. Carl Sweazy of the Arapahos described his tribe members chasing cattle as they used to do the buffalo, and bringing them down amidst cheers and celebrations. "For a few hours," Sweazy wrote in the 1890s, "the Arapaho knew once more some of the excitement of the buffalo hunt."[38]

The Great Western Trail's importance differed significantly in two important aspects from the other two prominent trails. Firstly, whereas the Shawnee and Chisholm Trails terminated at railheads, the Great Western Trail only made pit stops at railroad terminals. By the late 1880s, settlers had begun to establish large ranches in the northern territories – the Dakotas, Montana, and Wyoming – and needed Texas cattle to stock their ranges. Thus, many of the beeves on the Great Western Trail were driven further north to graze and mate. Secondly, after 1875, cattle drives came into Indian reservations (the reservation system was established in the Medicine Lodge Treaty of 1867) to sell cattle to the Plains Indians. The sale of cattle to the reservations proved to be a real slap in the face for Native Americans, too. For his efforts in containing Kiowa and Comanche attacks during the Civil War, the lands that comprised the canyons south of Amarillo, Texas were awarded to Charles Goodnight. This was traditionally Comanche and Kiowa land. Goodnight, who raised cattle on his new ranch, thus sold the Kiowas cattle grazed on their own land.

Texas Great Western Trail Tour (3 days)
San Antonio, Bandera, Bandera Pass, Kerrville, Harper, Yates, London, Menard, Brady, Santa Anna, Coleman, Baird, Buffalo Gap, Abilene, Albany, Fort Griffin, Throckmorton, Seymour, Vernon, and Doan's Crossing

In southern Texas, tracing the Great Western Trail is haphazard at best. Communities around San Antonio supplied cattle drives along numerous feeder trails, so an actual, delineated trail is not easy to locate until the trail reaches Fort Griffin. Therefore, you will start your tour in the gathering spot for many of the Great Western Trail drivers – San Antonio, one of the world's most culturally diverse cities.

During the trip through Texas you will be in quintessential cattle ranching county, as not much other productivity can be taken from the land. Natural landmarks will have decidedly "western" names: creeks and rivers are called "draws," the scrubby valleys around the scraggy hills are "hollows" or "gaps," and "Farm-to-Market Roads" are called "Ranch Roads." In the midst of the beautiful Texas Hill Country, you will also be in the center of frontier history, as many of the depredations committed by Indians against settlers occurred around the settlements along the Great Western Trail. One of the reasons Texas gave in 1861 for seceding from the Union was that the federal government was not providing settlers with the protection they needed – using this argument, Texas slave holders were able to convince westerners to get behind their cause.[39]

San Antonio
- Alamo and Mission District
- Hotels, gas stations, and restaurants

Directions:
You will begin your Great Western Tour at the famous Alamo, located north of the San Antonio Missions National Historic Park, at Alamo Plaza between East Houston and East Commerce Streets.
What's to See:
San Antonio is one of the oldest cities in the United States. As one of the northern-most Spanish colonial settlements, the city

began inside Mission San José (6519 San Jose Drive) in 1720. Within ten years, other missions followed, many re-located from eastern Texas to consolidate colonial administration: Mission San Juan Capistrano (9101 Graf Road), Mission San Francisco de la Espada (10040 Espada Road), and Mission Nuestra Señora de la Purísima Concepción de Acuña (807 Mission Road). In 1793, the Spanish gave control of the missions to the San Antonians, which they used for protection and churches. The missions can be visited by following the designated historic trail (well-marked) that hugs the San Antonio River.

Mission San Jose in San Antonio. Photo by author.

The jewel of San Antonio's historic structures is the Alamo. This storied edifice is only a ruin of a once larger mission that, after 1793, served as a military outpost for Spanish and Mexican troops. During the Texas Revolution, the Alamo was a fortified garrison in which Mexican troops were encamped.

In the 1830s, some Texans (American-born) and Tejanos (Mexican-born) voiced grievances against the Mexican government for curtailing American immigration, levying increased tariffs on what used to be a tariff-free zone, and outlawing slavery. By 1835, these complaints dissolved into an outright rebellion against Mexico. Texan troops conquered the Alamo, though under the famed general Santa Anna, Mexican troops re-seized it, and in the process killed hundreds of Texan army volunteers, including Davy Crockett and Jim Bowie. "Remember the Alamo!" became a rallying cry for subsequent battles, culminating in a victory for Texans at the Battle of San Jacinto in 1836.

After the revolution, however, no one remembered the Alamo much. The scarred ruin served as grain storage, Civil War quarters, and some-time church, and, at one point, was in danger of being razed. Through the efforts of concerned citizens and the Daughters of the Texas Revolution, San Antonio chapter, the Alamo has become one of Texas' most recognizable symbols.

San Antonio's growing importance as a trading, administrative, and religious center enticed Mexican, Native American, American, and European pioneers. After Texas independence (1836) and subsequent statehood (1845), several other nationalities came to San Antonio, including a large influx of German settlers. All of these cultural groups had one thing in common, and that was the desire to make money. Land speculation gave way to farming, ranching, and livestock handling. By the late 1860s, San Antonio became a cattle driving market for the Chisholm Trail and later, the Great Western Trail. When the railroads came through, the Union Stockyards, opened in 1889, shipped and processed thousands of cattle, pigs, and sheep (1716 San Marcos Drive). The stockyards closed in 2001.

Little of San Antonio's cattle driving past can be seen today. The city concentrates on its colonial history, romantic scenes like the Riverwalk (East Commerce), and new enticements like Sea World (Westover Hills Boulevard) and Six Flags (17000 Interstate 10).

Bandera
- Western history
- Hotels, gas stations, and restaurants

Directions:
1) From the Alamo in San Antonio, take East Crocket Street (facing west of Almao Plaza) to Loyosa Street. Turn left (south) onto Loyosa Street.
2) Turn right (west) onto East Commerce Street.
3) Turn right (north) onto San Saba Street.
4) Take ramp to merge onto Interstate 10/ US 87/ TX 564 (west). Follow this road for approximately 13 miles.
5) Take Exit 568B = TX 421/ Culebra Avenue. Turn left (west) onto TX 421/ Culebra Avenue.

6) After the intersection of TX 421/ Culebra Avenue and Wilson Boulevard, keep right to stay on TX 421/ Bandera Road. You will be heading northwest now.
7) Continue northwest for approximately 21 miles. TX 421/ Bandera Road becomes TX 16/ Bandera Road. Continue to follow TX 16/ Bandera Road for approximately 17 miles to Main Street/ TX 16/ TX 173 in downtown Bandera.
What's to See:
     Nestled next to the Medina River, Bandera is a small and cozy town with a proud western heritage. After the Civil War, many of the town's farmers turned into trail drivers, using the Old Spanish Trail (TX 173) to take the longhorns to market. Reflecting this history, saloons and dance halls – some original and some re-created - line the streets. The Frontier Museum (510 13th Street) tells the history of Bandera.

Bandera Pass and Camp Verde
- Old Spanish Road

Directions:
1) From Main Street/ TX 16/ TX 173 in Bandera, turn right (northeast) onto Sycamore Street/ TX 173.
2) Follow TX 173 north towards Kerrville. Mid-way is Bandera Pass, with a Great Western Trail Marker (on the west side of the road).
3) Approximately 10 miles further north is the Camp Verde General Store, which used to supply nearby Camp Verde (now in ruins).
What's to See:
     You will be following the road used by Spanish missionaries, conquistadors, and settlers as you wind your way up TX 173. Bandera Pass, used as a reference point for travelers on the road, is a narrow strip of land between two imposing mountains. The narrow gorge forced the cattle on the drives to pack tightly together to make their way through the gulley. While the pass poses no problem for today's visitor, it's easy to imagine how difficult the journey must have been for the trail drivers.
     North of Bandera Pass is the Verde Pass along the Verde River, with the ruins of Camp Verde nearby. Camp Verde served as a fort for brief periods between 1855 and 1869 and was also the site

of a much-discussed camel experiment. Jefferson Davis, who served as the Secretary of War prior to southern secession, imported 40 camels in the hopes of making travel and communication relays easier in the rocky, arid southwest. Nothing came out of this experiment, except for some interesting displays at the Camp Verde General Store and Bandera's Frontier Museum.

Kerrville
- German Heritage
- Hotels, gas stations, and restaurants

Directions:
1) From Camp Verde, continue north on TX 173 for approximately 12 miles until it ends at TX 16/ Sidney Baker Street.
2) Turn right (north) onto TX 16/ Sidney Baker Street to reach downtown Kerrville.

What's to See:
    Kerrville owes its name to James Kerr, one of Stephen F. Austin's "Original Three Hundred" who never even lived in Kerrville or Kerr County. Instead, a settler named Joshua D. Brown decided to bestow this honor on his old friend, though the area had probably already been named by the many Native Americans who called the valley around the Guadalupe River home.
    Kerrville boomed with a diversified economy both before and after the Civil War, activities which included cattle trailing and ranching. Today's Kerrville reflects very little of the cowboy era. Its main industries in cotton, timber, milling, and crafts, in addition to its large German heritage, instead recall Kerrville's prominence as the economic center of the Texas Hill Country.
    If you are interested in further exploring the impact of German settlers in Texas, visit nearby Fredericksburg (approximately 30 miles northeast on TX 16).

Harper, Yates, and London
- True western scenery and scenic river crossings

Directions:
1) From the courthouse in downtown Kerrville, follow Main Street/ TX 27 (right) northwest to Harper Road/ Ranch Road 783.
2) Turn right (northeast) onto Harper Road/ Ranch Road 783.

3) Follow Harper Road/ Ranch Road 783 for approximately 20 miles to Harper.
4) In Harper, turn left (west) onto US 290 and follow it for approximately 4 miles.
5) Turn right (north) onto Ranch Road 385. Follow this road for approximately 35 miles. On this stretch of road you will pass the old village of Yates near the Llano River.
6) Turn right (northeast) onto US 377.
7) Follow US 377 north to London.

The road will take you right over the cattle trail's Llano River Crossing. Photo by author.

What's to See:

Both Ranch Road 783 and Ranch Road 385 provide a strong visual interpretation of the Great Western Trail. Winding up, down, and around scrubby and rocky hills, the road can suddenly dip to cross over unpredictable streams that are subject to sudden flash flooding (take great caution in rainy weather).

Harper, the first town you will encounter, has served as a farm and ranch center since its inception in the 1860s.

A marker commemorating the "Old Beef Trail" sits at the scenic crossing of the Llano River in what used to be Yates.

The little town of London apparently enjoys its name very much, with several "London Pubs" clustered around US 377. London was a gathering point for feeder trails. The drives would then split in different directions, with some outfits trailing to

Menard; some through Marengo, or what is now called Hext; and some going towards Mason.

Just like England's London, Texas' version has a certain kind of charm. Photo by author.

Menard
- San Saba Mission and trail crossing
- Gas stations

Directions:
1) From London, follow US 377 northeast for approximately one mile northeast to Ranch Road 1221.
2) Turn left (north) onto Ranch Road 1221.
3) Continue north on Ranch Road 1221 for approximately 14 miles to Hext, which lies at the intersection of Ranch Road 1221 and TX 29.
4) Turn left (west) onto TX 29 towards Menard.
5) Near Menard, veer right (north) onto US 83 and follow US 83 into Menard.

What's to See:
Hext sits along one of the original Texas cattle roads. The nearby crossing at Cow Creek served as a watering station and trail intersection.

Menard has an extensive colonial past in spite of its non-Spanish name. Just two miles northwest of the town's center lie the ruins of the San Saba Presidio (Presidio San Luis de las Amarillas) where Spanish troops guarded the nearby mission (Hwy 190 West). The mission was raided and burned by Comanche, Toavayan, and Caddoan warriors in 1758, sparking a revenge mission commandeered by Diego Oritz Parilla. He and his relatively small contingent tracked the raiders all the way to the Red River, where they found the Native Americans ensconced in a large wooden fort. After a half-hearted attack, the Spanish troops were repelled, with the result that Spanish *colonistas* never ventured permanently into north Texas, fearing the northern Texas Indians which they called *norteños*. Spanish Fort, the American town that was founded on the battle site in the mid-19th century, became a prominent stop on the Chisholm Trail.

The wheel along Menard's "ditch." Photo by author.

Today, the San Saba Presidio sits alongside Menard's municipal golf course. Reconstructed on top of the original stone ruins in 1936, the new structure is now also in ruins. Cow Crossing Park, so named because the Great Western Trail crossed the San Saba River here, is a day-use facility with picnic benches and fishing posts (W. San Saba Avenue/ Ranch Road 2092).

Through downtown Menard runs the "historic ditch," a man-made water channel that has helped irrigate the town since the 1870s. A portion of the ditch can be walked.

Just west of Menard is Fort McKavett State Historical Park. Several buildings and ruins make up this day-use site, and historical reenactments occur in March. Further west lies picturesque Fort Concho National Historic Landmark in San Angelo.

Mason
- Trail history
- Gas stations and restaurants

Directions:
1) From Menard, backtrack on US 83 south to the junction with TX 29.
2) Veer left (east) onto TX 29. This road will take you back to Hext.
3) Continue east on TX 29 for approximately 30 miles.
4) Turn right (south) onto US 87/ TX 29/ Fort McKavitt Road.
5) Follow US 87/ TX 29/ Fort McKavitt Road into downtown Mason.

What's to See:

Mason grew out of an old Union fort, one of many that marked the "frontier line" of Texas settlement during the 1850s. It remained an active fort in the Civil War, albeit for the Confederate Army, who imprisoned Union sympathizers there.

After the Civil War, the fort returned to Union control, which helped to quell the numerous Indian raids in the area. After the Comanches, Kiowas, and Lipans were forced onto reservations in Indian Territory by 1875, the town of Mason then flourished as a cattle trading center.

Fort Mason is no more, as some of the more practical citizens used the fort's rock for building their own houses. Mason still has great things to visit, such as a very active bat cave, the Mason Square Museum (103 Fort McKavitt), the Mason County Historical Museum (Moody Street), and a picturesque downtown. An 1893 jail graces West Moreland Street. A statue on the courthouse square commemorates the area's ranchers and trail drivers. During Mason's frenetic post-war period, cowboys drove their cattle right through town.

Brady
- Museums
- Gas stations and restaurants

Directions:
1) From downtown Mason, take US 87 north for approximately 32 miles to downtown Brady. The road into downtown Brady is called Bridge Street.

What's to See:
Brady, seat of McCulloch county, is proud of being near the geographic center of Texas. An old livestock trading center, cattle on the Western Trail crossed near the town at Brady Creek. Visit the Heart of Texas Museum, located in the gothic old jail (117 N. High Street). Stop by the Soldier's Watering Hole (from US 190, take FM 412, go east two miles), where pioneers and soldiers would stop to rest and drink. Several unfortunate pioneers were massacred by Indians at the site in the early 1860s, and the victims are buried nearby.

Santa Anna
- Downtown
- Gas stations and restaurants

Directions:
1) From downtown Brady, follow West Commerce Street/ US 283/ TX 87.
2) Outside of Brady, veer right (north) to follow US 283 for approximately 45 miles to Santa Anna.

What's to See:
On US 283 north of Brady you will pass through Cow Gap near Table Top Mountain. Here, feeder trails from surrounding communities converged on their way to Coleman, including the Goodnight-Loving Trail, which headed west into New Mexico.

Santa Anna was named for a Comanche Chief, and not the Texans' revolutionary foe. In the 1880s, Santa Anna was home to the first female sheriff in Texas, who inherited the post from her husband. The downtown is very picturesque, in a dilapidated sort of way.

Coleman
- Downtown
- Gas stations and restaurants

Directions:
1) From Santa Anna, continue to follow US 283 for approximately 10 miles north to Coleman.
3) To reach downtown Coleman, turn left (west) onto Walnut Street and follow it to the intersection of Walnut Street and North Neches Street/ TX 206.

What's to See:
      Coleman, named after Sam Houston's aide Robert Coleman, lies on the picturesque Hord's Creek, which cattle forded on their way to the Kansas markets. The little town took full advantage of its location and boomed as a supply stop. Later, the town's brick making facility (now defunct) helped to build up the surrounding area, including the city's jail.
      To the east lies Brownwood, a supply stop for cattle drivers on feeder trails. Today, Brownwood is a busy county seat thanks to the railroads, cotton farming, and Howard Payne College.

Baird
- Railroad history

Directions:
1) From downtown Coleman, follow North Neches Street/ TX 206 north to the intersection with US 283.
2) Veer right, then jog left, to follow US 283 out of Coleman.
3) Follow US 283 north for approximately 41 miles to Baird. Road side trail markers will guide you along this path. You will notice that the landscape becomes a little flatter and wider in this section of Texas, too.
4) To reach downtown Baird, turn left (west) onto E 4th Street/ US 80.

What's to See:
      Baird, the seat of Callahan County, served as a supply stop on the Great Western Trail, but really grew with the arrival of the Texas Pacific Railway in the 1880s. The Texas and Pacific depot, which now houses city offices, stands at the southern end of town.
      Baird prides itself as being the "Antique Capital of West Texas," so if you want something old, you might just find it in Baird.

Abilene, Fort Phantom Hill and Buffalo Gap
- Museums and fort ruins
- Hotels, gas stations, and restaurants

Directions:
1) From downtown Baird, follow E. 4th Street/ US 80 west to the intersection with Interstate 20.

2) Turn left (west) to merge onto Interstate 20 and follow it for approximately 20 miles into downtown Abilene.
What's to See:

As the second largest city you will encounter in the Texas portion of the Great Western Trail, Abilene is definitely worth a look, albeit a short one. Because the city was built primarily by the railroad and speculators, it is more ranch than trail-oriented, but that doesn't stop the city from celebrating with cattle drive reenactments during its annual Western Heritage Classic, usually held in May.

Frontier Texas in downtown Abilene is an interactive, technological museum dedicated to recreating Western scenery and experiences (625 N. 1st Street). Eleven miles north of town is Fort Phantom Hill (FM 600), a scenic ruin of an antebellum frontier fort which, after it was abandoned, served as a stop and supply station for the Butterfield Overland Stagecoach Company. Later, it became a buffalo hide trading center, but was quickly abandoned after the buffalo herds were exterminated.

Nine miles southwest of Abilene lies the small village of Buffalo Gap (Sayles Boulevard to Buffalo Gap Road / FM 89). Despite being just south of the rather flat, sprawled-out vistas of Abilene, Buffalo Gap is shady, hilly, and compact, thanks to its location in the Callahan Divide. As it was the first town in Taylor County and was located along several important trading routes, Buffalo Gap became the first county seat and was also a supply stop for cattle trailers and buffalo hunters. It lost its bid to become Taylor County's permanent capital when Abilene was chosen as a hub for the Texas and Pacific Railroad. The Buffalo Gap Historic Village is an open air, living history museum displaying, among other things, a one-room school, a 1930s gas station, and the original Taylor County Courthouse and jail (133 William Street). The museum is self-guided and may take several very worthy hours to get through.

Nearby Buffalo Gap is scenic Abilene State Park, with ample camping and a CCC-built swimming pool.

Albany
- Museums
- Gas stations and restaurants

Directions:
1) From downtown Abilene, backtrack east on Interstate 20 to Baird.
2) Take Exit 307 = US 283.
3) Follow US 283 north for approximately 25 miles to Albany.

What's to See:

Albany had its beginnings as a rival to Fort Griffin Flat, a camp town located at the base of Fort Griffin (to the north). Albany-ians wanted the seat of Shackleford County to leave Fort Griffin Flat, a frontier town with a rough reputation. A few years later, Albany successfully won the right-of-way for the Texas and Pacific Railroad, cementing Fort Griffin Flat's destiny as a ghost town.

Albany is centered around an absolutely breathtaking courthouse. Nearby is the Old Jail Art Center, home to an impressive art collection (201 S. 2nd Street).

Fort Griffin and Fort Griffin Flat
- State Park and ghost town

Directions:
1) From Albany, follow US 283 north for approximately 11 miles to Fort Griffin State Park. The fort will be on the left (west) side of US 283. Camping facilities are located against the Brazos River inside a small park on the right (east) side of the highway. Ample signage will direct you.

Bridge across the Brazos River at Fort Griffin Flat. Photo by author.

What's to See:

A ruinous left-over from the days when American settlers feared the Comanches, Fort Griffin replaced the antebellum Camp Cooper, where none other than Robert E. Lee held one of his first commands. Along the Pease River just north of the fort, Peta Nocona, better known as Quanah Parker's father, met his death in a heated battle against American troops and ranchers. Famous cattle man Charles Goodnight depicted the battle scene in his memoirs.[40]

Fort Griffin is now a scenic, isolated ruin maintained by the Texas Historic Commission. On a dirt road just north of the entrance to the fort (along the base of the hillside), lie the remnants of Fort Griffin Flat, an outpost town that catered to the fort soldiers and later, to the cattle drivers. A calaboose, a recreated store, and a Great Western Trail marker line the dirt road.

Throckmorton and Seymour
- Downtowns
- Gas stations

Directions:
1) Fort Griffin State Park, continue driving north on US 283 for approximately 25 miles to Throckmorton.
2) From Throckmorton, continue north on US 283 for approximately 30 miles to Seymour.

What's to See:

Driving north on US 283, the landscape may surprise you, with its large hills, tall prairie grasses, and scenic creeks and streams. On your way, you will pass through the little town of Throckmorton, county seat of Throckmorton County.

Seymour served as a supply stop and camping ground for trail drivers. Cattle forded the Seymour Creek, a tributary of the Brazos River, inside today's Seymour's City Park. US 82, which runs as California Street through the center of Seymour, is the California Gold Rush road that Randalph B. Marcy laid out in the early 1850s.

Vernon
- Museum
- Hotels, gas stations, and restaurants

Directions:
1) From Seymour, drive northeast on US 283/ US 82/ US 277/ US 183 to Mabelle.
2) In Mabelle, turn right (north) to follow US 283 for approximately 36 miles to Vernon.
3) In Vernon, US 283 is also Main Street, which will lead you into downtown Vernon.

What's to See:
  Before the official creation of Vernon, this town was called Eagle Spring by the Tonkawas and Eagle Flat by settlers. The post office refused both names, and the name Vernon was picked (either as homage to Mount Vernon or in (dubious) honor of a traveling whiskey salesman). Vernon served as a stop on the Great Western Trail during the latter part of the drives.
  The Red River Valley Museum (4600 College Drive) is an excellent resource, filled with displays pertaining to the Great Western Trail, ranching, the 1979 tornado outbreak, and Cynthia Ann Parker. The museum is funded in part by the Waggoner Ranch family, which owns most of the surrounding land, and is accordingly well outfitted. Downtown Vernon has many old buildings, and some cool vintage signage. North of Vernon on US 283 is a cement and sandstone marker commemorating the Western Trail, which ran right alongside the highway.

Doan's Crossing
- Ghost town

Directions:
1) From downtown Vernon, follow US 283 north out of town for approximately 13 miles.
2) Turn right (east) onto Ranch Road 924 at Fargo.
3) Follow Ranch Road 924 to Doan's Crossing, which lies at the intersection of Ranch Roads 924 and 2916.

What's to See:
  Doan' Crossing is a remarkable relic of the past. The town began as a supply stop for cattle drivers, and grew into a thriving trading center near the Red River. Hundreds of people, including Quanah Parker and John Lytle, and thousands of cattle visited the wooden and adobe buildings along Main Street during the cattle drives, but the town died when the railroad favored Vernon. Today,

only an original 1881 adobe store, built by Corwin Doan, remains. Descendants of towns people keep up the small building and its outhouse, as Doan's serves as a reunion site and school field trip destination. Several historical markers commemorate what Doan's Crossing once was. Doan's Crossing is the last stop on the Texas leg of the Great Western Trail tour.

Thousands of cattle crossed the Red River at Doan's store. Photo by author.

Oklahoma Great Western Trail Tour (2 days)
Altus, Friendship, Warren, Granite, Lone Wolf, Old Retrop, Retrop, Port, Elk City, Canute, Foss, Edwardsville, Butler, Leedey, Trail, Carmago, Vici, Woodward, Fargo, Fort Supply, May, Laverne, Buffalo, Doby Springs, and Yelton

Whereas the Shawnee and Chisholm Trails ran through lands owned by the Five Civilized Tribes, the Great Western Trail crossed lands occupied by Plains inhabitants: the Comanches, Kiowas, Apaches, Arapahos, and Cheyennes. After the Southern Plains Indians were forced onto reservations, drivers would ask for military escorts so as not to be forced to give all their cattle to bands who demanded cows as toll. While sparsely inhabited, the Great Western Trail, which was called the Texas or Lone Star Trail by Oklahomans, offered some respite for the drivers in the form of scattered trading posts and several camp grounds with fresh water springs. However, most of the towns described in this section are "Sooner" settlements, and reflect farm rather than ranch heritages.

This tour follows along the remains of the last long distance cattle drives, which occurred in the 1890s. By this time, what would become the state of Oklahoma had split into two separate territories – the eastern Indian Territory, which was reserved for Native American tribes, and the western Oklahoma Territory, which had been set aside for other settlers.

The most interesting sights along the Great Western Trail in Oklahoma have less to do with the trail than with the remnants of another historical event: the Dust Bowl. Along this journey, you will see many abandoned farms left from the Great Depression, wind-blown prairies, forgotten ghost towns along country roads, tree shelter lines planted by the CCC in the 1930s, and boarded up schools.

Altus
- Railroad history
- Hotels, gas stations, and restaurants

Directions:
1) From Doan's Crossing, take Ranch Road 2916 west to US 283.
2) Turn right (north) onto US 283 and follow that road for approximately 20 miles into Altus, Oklahoma. In Altus, US 283 becomes Main Street.

What's to See:

While Altus, founded in 1895, is not an original trail town, its location did serve as a watering hole for cattle. Cowboys called the future site of Altus "Buttermilk Creek," as early settlers sold them fresh buttermilk. Today, Altus is one of the larger cities in southwestern Oklahoma, with a university and an air force base. The original depot and loading area, which is partially paved with Thurber brick, still stands just west of Main Street. Altus once even changed its name to Leger to honor a railroad contractor's wife. The city resumed its old name once the rails were built, however. North of the square, the town expands with many restaurants and shopping opportunities as it serves as a gateway to the Wichita Mountains.

Friendship, Warren, Granite, and Lone Wolf
- Trail history

Directions:
1) From downtown Altus, keep north on US 283/ Main Street. The following place names are listed in geographical order, from southern-most to northern-most. There's not much to see in these little towns, so skipping some of them would not disrupt your journey.
2) To arrive at Friendship, turn right (east) onto E1600 Road (across from the Altus-Quartz Mountain Regional Airport). Follow E1600 Road for approximately 2 miles to Friendship.
3) To find Warren from Friendship, take N2100 Road north to OK 19, then turn right (east) at Warren.
4) To reach Lone Wolf from Warren, take OK 19 west to the intersection of OK 19 and US 283. Turn right (north) onto US 283, then veer to the right to follow OK 44 north. Continue north on OK 44 for approximately 15 miles to OK 9 in Lone Wolf. You will pass through Quartz Mountain State Park, which is worth a visit.
5) To locate Granite from Lone Wolf, follow OK 9 west for approximately 8 miles to Granite. In Granite, turn right at OK 6 to reach downtown.

What's to See:

North of Altus, the trail deviates very much from the thoroughfares. Running east of US 283, it continues in a zig-zag pattern, skirting the Wichita Mountains and passing near land rush towns like Friendship, Warren, Granite, and Lone Wolf.

Remnants of the past in Lone Wolf. Photo by author.

In Friendship, the Friendship Store was a supply stop directly on the trail. The store is long gone, but a historical marker has been placed near where it once stood.

The trail passed less than a mile east of Warren. Close by, a fresh water well served the trail drivers at a camping site. North of Warren lie several mountains. Drivers going up the trail navigated their way using the tallest one, Teepee Mountain.

Lone Wolf sits just east of the trail. It's a cute little town with an orange water tower and an old blacksmith shop.

Between Lone Wolf and Granite is Quartz Mountains State Park, which surrounds old Lake Altus. Granite sits at the southern tip of the Headquarters Mountains, where both trail drivers and soldiers, who were employed to guard the trail drives, camped.

Retrop, Old Retrop, and Port
- Ghost towns

Directions:
1) In Granite, follow OK 6 north for approximately 15 miles to Retrop.
2) To reach to Old Retrop from Retrop, turn right (east) onto OK 55, then turn right (south) onto N2040 Road. Follow N2040 Road one mile south to Old Retrop.
5) To access Port from Old Retrop, take N2040 Road one mile north to OK 55. Turn right (east) onto OK 55 and follow it for approximately 2 miles. Turn left (north) onto N2060 Road and follow it for approximately 3 miles to E1250 Road. Port lies at the intersection of N2060 Road and E1250 Road.

What's to See:

Old Retrop used to be just plain Retrop until the town's citizens moved closer to the highway junctions. Today, (new) Retrop is a small crossroads town. And Retrop used to be called Porter, until the post office application was rejected it. The town's citizens, savvy as they were, just reversed the spelling.

Old Retrop, just a mile to the east of Retrop, sits directly on the trail, but it's not a trail town. Begun as a small farming community, the Dust Bowl helped to wipe it out. The old town center, consisting of a store, cemetery, and abandoned farm buildings, sits along a country road.

The trail crossed directly at Port, a miniscule spot on the map (though it did once have a post office) just northeast of Old Retrop. To the north is Soldiers Spring (private property), where both trail drivers and soldiers found a fresh water source amidst the arid, windswept prairie. Nothing of note remains at Port.

Old Retrop's downtown. Photo by author.

Elk City
- Route 66 History and museums
- Hotels, gas stations, and restaurants

Directions:
1) From Port, take E1250 west for approximately 6 miles to the intersection with OK 6.
2) Turn right (north) onto OK 6 and follow it for approximately 14 miles to Elk City. Once in Elk City, OK 6 becomes Main Street.

What' to See:

Elk City formally began in 1907 as a land rush town and has grown into a fairly large city thanks to its location along Route 66. The national highway brought commerce and tourists to this town on the prairie and is still its main thoroughfare. Several museums, all within the Old Town Museum complex, commemorate Elk City's history (2717 Highway 66). Tourists are particularly fond of the National Route 66 Museum in the museum complex, which celebrates all eight Route 66 states with memorabilia and photographs. Other interesting museums in the complex include the Old Town Museum, which is housed in a Victorian mansion; the Transportation Museum that displays old fire fighting equipment; and an outdoor Farm and Ranch Museum with living history demonstrations.

Canute, Foss, Edwardsville, and Butler
- Route 66 sites, ghost towns, and trail history
- Gas stations and restaurants

Directions:
1) From downtown Elk City, turn right (east) onto Historic Route 66/ 3rd Street/ OK 34/ OK 40. Follow this road for approximately 3 miles to the intersection with Interstate 40.
2) Follow Interstate 40 east for approximately 6 miles to Exit 47 = Canute.
3) To reach Foss from Canute, continue east on Interstate 40 for approximately 5 miles to Exit 53 = Foss. Turn left (north) onto OK 44 and follow it for approximately 2 miles into Foss.
4) The old town of Edwardsville now lies under Foss Lake, which sits between Foss and Butler along OK 44.
5) To visit Butler from Foss, continue north on OK 44 for approximately 14 miles to the intersection of OK 33.

What's to See:

Canute, Foss, and Butler are land rush towns situated almost directly on the trail.

Canute's stretch of Route 66 includes an early 1940s service station that the National Register of Historic Places listed as "an excellent example of the southwestern adaptation of the art deco architectural style known as pueblo deco."[41]

While some residents remain in Foss, Interstate 44 has siphoned so much of its business that today, Foss can be considered a ghost town.

Between Foss and Butler lies the trail town of Edwardsville, which was established in 1889. Edwardsville is no more, having succumbed to the waters of Foss Lake. Foss Lake has also swallowed General Custer's 1875 camp site. 1875 wasn't the first time Custer traversed this country; he and his men came through in 1868, when they were tracking Black Kettle and his Cheyenee tribe. That same year, Custer killed Black Kettle at what became known as the Washita Battle, now a National Historic Site west of Foss Lake inside the Black Kettle National Grasslands.

Near Butler is Soldier Camp, a sandstone outcrop on which trail drivers and soldiers carved messages and initials, though the rock is not visible anymore.

Leedey, Trail, Carmago, and Vici
- Trail and frontier history
- Gas stations and restaurants

Directions:
1) From Butler, follow OK 33 west for approximately 12 miles to Hammon, Oklahoma.
2) In Hammon, turn right (north) onto OK 34.
3) Continue north on OK 34 for approximately 17 miles to Leedey.
3) To reach Trail from Leedey, follow OK 34 north to E0720 Road. Trail sits just east of OK 34 at the junction of E0720 Road and N2080 Road. While there's no trace of Trail anymore, the Canadian River bends just a mile east of the former townsite.
4) To visit Carmargo from Trail, back track to OK 34. Follow OK 34 north for approximately 11 miles to Carmargo.
5) To arrive at Vici from Camargo, follow OK 34 north for approximately 11 miles to Vici.

What's to See:
Leedey does not sit directly on the trail, but the town does sport a great reminder of frontier justice: a sturdy and tidy calaboose, complete with a metal, wall-mounted toilet, sits on the west side of Highway 34.

Frontier business in Leedey. Photo by author.

The aptly named town of Trail even had a post office at one point, but now there's not really anything there at all.

Carmago is less than a mile north of the Canadian River. Before it was a town, Carmago was the site of a buffalo river crossing that turned into a trail crossing. Old timers locate the actual trail crossing at the old Missouri-Kansas-Texas Railroad bridge in Carmago, which has since been torn down. Just west of the Canadian River, between Carmago and Vici, the trail drivers rested at Cedar Springs, which flow on a private farm.

Vici is yet another farm community, but trail history is visible west of town. Follow US 60/ OK 51 west for approximately 4 miles to a large granite trail marker on the south side of the road. The Great Western Trail is still fairly visible in the tall grass prairie landscape.

Woodward and Fargo
- Trail history and museum
- Hotels, gas stations, and restaurants

Directions:
1) From Vici, continue north on OK 34 for approximately 18 miles to Woodward. Downtown Woodward sits at the junction of Ok 34 and OK 15.
2) To locate Fargo from Woodward, turn left (west) onto Oklahoma Avenue / OK 15 and follow it for approximately 15 miles to Fargo.

What's to See:

Woodward began as a supply point for soldiers at nearby Fort Supply, and developed into a cattle trading center when the railroads came through in the early 20th century. Woodward is still a prominent farming and ranching center. Its history is recounted at the Plains Indians and Pioneer Museum (2009 Williams Avenue).

Fargo is the home of Boggy Creek, where trail drivers would rest and bed their cattle. A nice park and historical marker on the east side of Fargo commemorate this history. Just north of Fargo is the old John Smith Farm at Horseshoe Lake and spring, where the drivers forded Wolf Creek.

Fort Supply
- Frontier history

Directions:
1) From Fargo, backtrack to Woodward east on OK 15.
2) In Woodward, turn left (north) to follow NW Highway Street/ US 270/ US 183/ US 412/ OK 3 north for approximately 15 miles to Fort Supply.

What's to See:
Established as a supply fort for the campaigns against the Southern Plains Indians in 1868, Fort Supply served as the prison for Black Kettle's Cheyenne bands after their defeat by General George Armstrong Custer. Soldiers from the fort sometimes escorted cattle drivers through the area, where Cheyenne and Arapaho hostilities ran deep against the drivers. The trail itself ran well west of the fort, as the cattle could be destructive to the cultivated fields. The fort was abandoned in 1894 after the land rush, and thereafter became Oklahoma's first state mental institution in 1908. Since 1988, a minimum security prison occupies the grounds, so make sure to lock your car and take your purse when you visit.

Fort Supply displays Kiowa ledger art. Photo of drawing by author.

When you enter the fort, follow the signs to the historic structures, which are quite impressive. Try not to stare too hard at all the prison-striped inmates glaring back at you.

May and Laverne
- Trail and railroad history
- Gas stations and restaurants

Directions:
1) From Fort Supply, take US 270/ US 412/ OK 3 northwest for approximately 10 miles to May.
2) To reach Lavern from May, take US 270/ US 412/ OK 3 west. Turn right (north) onto US 283, and follow US 283 into Laverne.

What's to See:
While these towns are not contemporaries of the trail, they do show remnants of the trail in the form of an old railroad bed. The tracks from the Wichita Falls and Northwestern Railway are now long gone, but their ghostly impressions approximate the trail through this portion of the country. Trail drivers who recounted their histories for the Federal Writer's Project in the 1930s used these towns to estimate where the old trail used to be.

Both towns were probably named after the wives or daughters of prominent railroad men. Rail history is well accounted for in Laverne, where the National Register of Historic Places lists several properties relating to the town's railroad heritage. Interestingly, the socialist newspaper *Beacon Light* was published in Laverne.

Buffalo, Doby Springs and Yelton
- Trail history
- Gas stations and restaurants

Directions:
1) From Laverne, follow US 283 west for approximately 8 miles to the intersection with US 64. 2) Turn right (east) onto US 64 and follow it for approximately 15 miles to Buffalo.
2) In Buffalo, turn left (north) onto N1830 Road. Signs will point you towards the Doby Springs Golf Course (semi-paved).
3) Continue north on N1830 for approximately 8 miles to the Kansas border.

What's to See:
Harper County, of which the town of Buffalo is the county seat, hosts a varied history. An original "soddie," which is an earthen pioneer houses, still stands. One of the most important archeological sites in North America, the Bison Kill Site, is also

located in Harper County. Excavations unearthed a painted bison skull, which proved to be one of the earliest examples of art in the continent. Both sites are restricted and inaccessible to visitors.

Buffalo Springs, a local water source, was renamed Doby Springs when its post office was opened in 1908. Today, the municipal golf course of Buffalo surrounds the springs.

You will not find Yelton on any modern map. It was a ghost town as early as 1936, when WPA historians began tracing the trail. Back in the trail days, Yelton was home to the Fair Store and Saloon.

As you drive north on this country road, you are directly on the Great Western Trail. This is the first and only time on this road trip that you have the opportunity to easily follow the actual trail. While fenced farms and ranches have taken over the landscape, try to imagine what it looked like over 120 years ago, when the range was still open, the prairie grasses abundant, and the buffalo thundered across the mysteriously beautiful Great Plains.

The Trail in Kansas (1 day)
Deep Hole Crossing, Ashland, Big Basin and St. Jacob's Well, Minneola, and Dodge City

The sparsely inhabited southern plains of Kansas still show signs of a pioneer past. Unlike the history of the southeast side of the state, southwest Kansas did not experience the bloody sectional wars, nor were sod-busters (a.k.a. homesteaders, nesters, farmers) sabotaging the cattle drives. By the time the Western Trail gained momentum in Kansas, the Southern Plains Indians were not even a threat anymore; settlers, soldiers, and speculators had unceremoniously pushed them out of their homelands and into Indian Territory.

What precipitated the Western Trail can be evidenced by what the landscape in Kansas lacks: the buffalo. Scores of buffalo hunters arrived as the railroad pushed its way into Dodge City. Getting at the most $3 per hide, the buffalo hunters slaughtered hundreds of thousands of bison to make room for the railroad, the cattle ranches, and the speculators – and to rid the countryside of the Native Americans. People all over the country were outraged at this practice, and though several congressmen and Americans tried to stop the slaughter, within a ten year period the entire Southwestern buffalo herds were exterminated.[42]

The drive to Dodge City had two major geographic hurtles for the cowboys: the Cimarron River crossing and the wind-swept caverns of the Big Basin.

The Cimarron River crossing is marked by a Great Western post. Photo by author.

Deep Hole Crossing
- Trail History

Directions:
1) From the Oklahoma and Kansas border, continue north on N1830 Road, which is named River Road in Kansas, to the Cimarron River crossing.

What's to See:
The trail crossed the Cimarron River alongside the small bridge – trail drivers named the passage "Deep Hole Crossing," though no major depressions were apparent. However, two saloons met the cowboys on the river, so maybe that's where the crossing got its name? These "watering holes" even sported names straight out of western dime novels: the Longhorn Round-Up Saloon and the Dead Fall Saloon.

Though the river looks narrow, shallow, and placid today, it could rage out of control very easily during the trail days, before rivers were dammed for flood control. On the east side of the bridge sits a cement marker designating the Great Western Trail crossing.

When you reach this crossing, get out of the car. Walk around and marvel at the beautiful landscape around you. Stare at the waters of the Cimarron – you might see a fossil or two – and discover what it is that makes Kansas so very special: the contrasting light, the wide horizons, and the immense dome of its sky.

Strangely, Zebulon Pike, the intrepid explorer hired by Thomas Jefferson to explore the Central Plains after the Louisiana Purchase, called this landscape "the Great American Desert."

Ashland
- Trail history
- Hotel, gas stations and restaurants

Directions:
1) From Deep Hole Crossing, continue north on River Road to Ashland. River Road becomes called Kentucky Road once you enter Ashland.
2) Kentucky Road ends at US 160 in Ashland.

What's to See:
Ashland was the first town of note that the trail drivers came across after leaving Texas and crossing Indian Territory. The town began when Bear Creek Mail Station was built in the 1870s, not long after the last of the Southern Plains buffalo herds had been exterminated. Ashland, a former stage coach stop, is the seat of Clark County. As you enter the town from River Road, note the quaint tourist court on US 160 – Ashland was a good place for the trail drivers to camp and apparently, it's still a good place to put one's feet up.

The trail took a more straight line north to Dodge City. Alas, there are no paved roads north of Ashland – you'll have to deviate from the trail considerably. The roads you will take for this last leg of the tour, however, still tell the story of what the cattle drivers experienced.

Big Basin and St. Jacob's Well

Directions:

1) From Kentucky Road in Ashland, turn left (west) onto US 160 and travel for approximately 18 miles to US 283.

2) Turn right (north) onto US 283. Follow US 283 for approximately 10 miles. You will see the entrance to the basins on either side of US 283.

What's to See:

US 160 west of Ashland slices through an astounding landscape, where red sandstone rock ledges prominently force their way out of the prairie grasses. This vista constitutes the edge of the Big and Little Basins.

The Big and Little Basins are geological anomalies – basically, they are huge sink holes on the flat plain that expose the red rock underneath. Trail drivers skirted this great divide to the east.

The haunting landscape of the Big Basin epitomizes the beauty and isolation of the Great Plains. Photo by author.

At the Big and Little Basins, the Kansas Department of Parks and Wildlife has set aside a few acres so that visitors can experience the strangeness of this place first hand. The roads are passable into both basins (not in a motor home, however). A buffalo herd has been re-established in the basins. They are free to roam around, and enjoy staring and snorting at visitors.

One mile east of the entrance to the Little Basin is St Jacob's Well, a deep watering hole that prehistoric people, Native Americans, pioneers, and cattle drivers frequented in this desolate landscape. Beware of the incredible plains winds that race through the basin!

Minneola
- Nearby history
- Gas stations and restaurants

Directions:
1) From the Big and Little Basins, continue to travel north on US 283 for approximately 10 miles to Minneola.

What's to See:
Minneola can thank its existence to the railroad, when it came through in 1887. As the tracks bypassed an earlier community named Appleton, citizens just packed up and moved to Minneola.

Nearby Meade (US 160 west) hosts a museum at a reputed Dalton Gang Hideout.

South of Minneola on US 283 are the ghostly remains of Englewood, established in 1884. While people still call this little township home, the many buildings left to rot along the main thoroughfares attest to a once busier place that may have been a supply stop for drivers on the Great Western Trail.

Dodge City
- Fort Dodge, Boot Hill Cemetery, Dead Line, Santa Fe Trail, railroad history, western history
- Hotels, gas stations, and restaurants

Directions:
1) From Minneola, continue driving north on US 283 for approximately 20 miles to Dodge City.
2) At the intersection of US 283 and US 56, travel straight to follow South 2nd Avenue into downtown Dodge City.
3) Downtown Dodge City is located where South 2nd Avenue meets Wyatt Earp Boulevard/ US 50.

What's to See:
Check it out – you've made it! Give your horse a well-deserved apple.

The trail drivers crossed the Arkansas River roughly in the same area where you will cross it along South 2nd Avenue (Wright Park). When you come into town, you will immediately witness the low slung buildings and dark beer halls that tell of a rough frontier heritage – the south side of Dodge City has always been the "anything goes" part of town. Needing a respectable town center, the town fathers divided Dodge City between the railroad tracks, and called the division the "Dead Line." North of the Dead Line stood upstanding businesses and stores. South of it, one could find notorious saloons, brothels, and maybe get caught up in a gunfight or two.[43] Gunfights were actually quite rare, however. Men were asked to check their weapons with the city marshal, as gun control was strictly enforced in Dodge City.

The Dodge City of the 20th century teemed with culture. Photo by author.

Fort Dodge, a pioneer protection and supply fort on the Santa Fe Trail, anchored Dodge City. The fort sits east of the town along the railroad tracks, which parallel the Santa Fe Trail. That famous trail brought buffalo hunters from the east, whose main occupation was to rid the plains of the buffalo and hence, the Indians. While the cattle drives proved to be Dodge City's ticket to fame and fortune, one must always remember that this Kansas outpost began for a violent, bloody, and inexcusable reason – to exterminate an eco system.

The first stop for any tourist to Dodge City is the Visitor's Bureau, located inside a converted train station (400 West Wyatt

Earp Boulevard). Then, take a walking tour through downtown. Running parallel to the north of Wyatt Earp Boulevard is the famous Front Street, Dodge City's original town center.

Unfortunately, Dodge City became a victim of the 1960s-1970s urban renewal projects. All of its brick buildings dating from the 1880s (the original wooden buildings succumbed to fires in the 1870s) were demolished along historic Front Street and today, a parking lot and the widened Wyatt Earp Boulevard occupy the original town site. Dodge City's famous Boot Hill cemetery also succumbed to urbanization. In the early 20th century, the cemetery was moved to make way for City Hall. The cemetery's original location is now the Boot Hill Museum Complex, which recreates Dodge City's Front Street (Front Street and Wyatt Earp Boulevard). A preserved portion of the Boot Hill Cemetery remains at the museum.

About five miles east from the Dodge City Visitor's Center is Fort Dodge, where several intact stone buildings still stand inside what is now, fittingly, the Kansas Veterans Retirement Home. Nine miles west of Dodge City on Wyatt Earp Boulevard/ U.S. 50, some of the best ruts on the Santa Fe Trail are preserved.

Wyatt Earp Boulevard, named after the legendary Dodge City marshal, is equally known by two other famous names. One can call it the Santa Fe Trail, which took pioneers from St. Louis to New Mexico in the 19th century. Or one can say it's the Lincoln Highway (US 50), a network of roads which constituted the earliest transcontinental highway in the United States.

End of the Great Western Trail

What makes traveling the Great Western Trail so different from other road trips is that the trail takes you back in time to several different points in history. Not only can you witness the cattle drives, but also the Indian wars and Depression-era America. Along the trail, you can experience first hand how Americans, in their quest for land and profit, tried to change the landscape, and how the land fought back.

Epilogue

The trailing of cattle through Texas, Oklahoma, and Kansas has become one of the defining events in American history. Americans have built their cultural image around the trails, but while America loves to glorify its past, it also neglects it.

Small towns are losing population to the big cities. Family farms and ranches are being incorporated into the large conglomerate operations. The railroads have consolidated and many tracks lay unused. Old, dusty cemeteries are slowly being forgotten. Historic buildings are demolished for parking lots, and some towns have been abandoned. The rivers have been diverted into lakes, and fences have long replaced the open range. New roads have obliterated most traces of the old trails.

As I travel along the routes of the old cattle drivers, I try to imagine how things used to be, before life became so hectic and modern… but then I realize that not much has changed. The truth is that the people who drove the cattle did not find their life simple or peaceful. Just like we do today, they were working for the money. The outfits were never comprised of "rugged individualists" but were business partnerships that sold their product (cattle) to corporations, who in turn invested in the railroads that later bypassed the old trail towns and forged new paths. The cattle trails were simply the forerunners of the modern shipping business and the dehumanization of the meat industry, and used low-paid labor to make all of this happen.

So why is there still such a fascination? I wager that the excitement comes from a need to understand America's brief, but incredibly fast-paced, past. So much of American history has been destroyed or distorted in such a relatively short time. If we can recognize just a little bit of what used to be, and connect it with an honest retelling of what was, then we might become better acquainted with the United States in general. That is what the mystique of the cattle drives offers the traveler: a chance to learn who Americans were and how the country grew into what it is now. Through these well-worn paths, one can see how the past influenced the present, and how, just maybe, we can fit into that picture ourselves. So what are you waiting for? Get in the car – on a bike – on a bus – on your own two feet – and go exploring!

Resources

Recommended Books

Drago, Harry Sinclair. *Great American Cattle Trails* (New York: Bramhall House, 1965).
- Drago helped to define the historic treatment of the American west with this comprehensive book.

Gard, Wayne. *The Chisholm Trail* (Norman: University of Oklahoma Press, 1954).
- Gard's research on the Chisholm Trail remains a mainstay for trail historians.

Hunter, Marvin J. (ed). *The Trail Drivers of Texas* [1924] (Austin: The University of Texas Press, 1985).
- By offering anecdotes and stories of several trail drivers, this 1000-page tome is a major resource for trail researchers.

Iverson, Peter. *When the Indians Became Cowboys: Native peoples and Cattle Ranching in the American West* (Norman: University of Oklahoma Press, 1994).
- A surprisingly revealing book on a little known of aspect of history: the Native American influence on cattle ranching and herding.

Krell, Alan. *The Devil's Rope: A Cultural History of Barbed Wire* (London: Reaktion Books, 2002).
- Learn all you can about barbed wire, and then some. Krell includes technical as well as historic information that transcends the American West.

Skaggs, Jimmy M. *The Cattle-Trailing Industry: Between Supply and Demand, 1866-1890* (Norman: University of Oklahoma Press, 1973).
- Skaggs' book is a thorough, economic treatment of the southwestern cattle drives.

Webb, Walter Prescott. *The Great Plains* (Boston: Ginn and Company, 1931).
- The seminal study on the history, ecology, climate, and impact of the Great Plains remains a leader in the study of the American West.

Recommended Websites

American Life Stories: Manuscripts from the Federal Writers' Project, 1936-1940 at the Library of Congress
http://memory.loc.gov/ammem/wpaintro/wpahome.html
- You may spend hours reading accounts of those who lived through slavery, pioneering, and cattle driving. Narrow your search to find authentic cowboy and cowgirl voices.

Indian- Pioneer Papers at University of Oklahoma Digital Library
- Compiled by workers of the Federal Writers' Project (under the Works Progress Administration in the 1930s), the Indian-Pioneer Papers provide insight into the industrialization, settlement, and politics of Indian Territory from the 1870s until statehood in 1907.

On the Chisholm Trail by Glen Sieber
http://www.thechisholmtrail.com
- Educational and just plain fun resource for everything related to the Chisholm Trail.

The Great Western Trail by various Texas tourist organizations
http://greatwesterncattletrail.com
- This site offers history and accommodation information for the Texas portions of the Great Western Trail.

The Shawnee Trail by various Texas tourist organizations
http://theshawneetrail.com
- This site offers history and accommodation information for the Texas portions of the Shawnee Trail.

Recommended Maps

Kansas Atlas & Gazeteer (DeLorme Publishing)
Missouri Atlas & Gazeteer (DeLorme Publishing)
Oklahoma Atlas & Gazeteer (DeLorme Publishing)

Oklahoma, the Roads of (Mapsco Publishing)
Texas Atlas & Gazeteer (DeLorme Publishing)
Texas, the Roads of (Mapsco Publishing)
Texas, the Roads of (Texas A&M University and Cartographic Division)

Resources on the Shawnee Trail
(alphabetical)

Baxter Springs Heritage Center and Museum
Admission charged, free parking
http://www.baxterspringsmuseum.org
740 East Ave, Baxter Springs, KS 66713 (620)856-2385

Boggy Depot State Park
Free admission, camping and RV hook ups available
475 S Park Lane, Atoka, OK 74525 (580)889-5625

Dallas Convention and Visitors Bureau
http://www.visitdallas.com

Five Civilized Tribes Museum
Admission charged, free parking
http://www.fivetribes.org
1109 Honor Heights Drive, Muskogee, OK 74401 (918)683-1701

Fort Gibson National Historic Site
Admission charged, free parking
http://www.fortgibson.com
907 N. Garrison, Fort Gibson, OK 74434 (918)478-4088

Fort Washita State Historic Park
Free admission, free parking
http://www.okhistory.org/outreach/military/fortwashita.html
3348 State Rd. 199 Durant, OK 74701 (580)924-6502

Frisco Heritage Museum
Admission charged, free parking
http://www.friscomuseum.com
6455 Page Street, Frisco, TX 75034 (972)292-5665

Eisenhower Birthplace State Historical Park
Admission charged, free parking

http://www.visiteisenhowerbirthplace.com
609 S. Lamar Avenue, Denison, TX 75021 (903)465-8908

High School Museum (with Coal Miner's Museum)
Admission charged, free parking
220 E. Adams, McAlester, OK 74502 (918)423-2932

Honey Springs Battle Site
Free admission, free parking
1863 Honey Springs Battlefield Rd, Checotah, OK 74426 (918)473-5572

Interurban Railway Museum
Suggested donation, free parking
901 E. 15th Street, Plano, TX 75074 (972)941-2117

Jesse James House Museum
Admission charged, free parking
http://www.ponyexpressjessejames.com
Penn Street and Mitchell Avenue, St. Joseph, MO (816) 232-8206

Kansas City Convention and Visitors Bureau
http://www.visitkc.com

Krebs Heritage Museum
Admission charged, free parking
85 South Main, McAlester, OK 74502 (918)426-0377

Loy Lake Park
Admission charged, free parking
Hwy 75, Loy Lake Road (Exit 67), Sherman, TX

North Texas History Center
Admission charged, free parking
http://www.northtexashistorycenter.org
300 E. Virginia, McKinney, TX 75069 (972)542-9457

Old Red Courthouse Museum
Admission charged, parking fees
http://www.oldred.org
100 S. Houston Street, Dallas, TX 75202 (214)745-1100

Pattee House Museum
Admission charged, free parking
http://www.ponyexpressjessejames.com
1202 Penn Street, St. Joseph, MO 64506 (816)232-8206

Plano Heritage Homestead Museum
Admission charged, free parking
http://www.heritagefarmstead.org
1900 West 15th Street, Plano, TX 75075 (972)881-0141

Pony Express National Museum
Admission charged, free parking
http://www.ponyexpress.org
914 Penn Street, St. Joseph, MO (800)530-5930

Red River Historical Museum
Suggested donation of $2, free parking
http://hosting.texoma.net/rrhms/frames.htm
301 S. Walnut Street, Sherman, TX 75090 (903)893-7623

Red River Railroad Museum
Suggested donations, free parking
http://www.redriverrailroadmuseum.org
101 E. Main Street, Denison, TX 75021 (903)463-KATY

Robbers Cave State Park
Free admission, free parking
Highway 2 North, Wilburton, OK 74578 (918)465-2565

Sedalia Visitors Center
Free admission, free parking
http://www.sedaliachamber.com
600 East 3rd Street, Sedalia, MO 65301 (660)826-2222

Three Valley Museum
Free admission, free parking
401 W. Main Street, Durant, OK 74701 (580)920-1907

Three Rivers Museum
Admission charged, free parking
http://3riversmuseum.com
220 Elgin Street, Muskogee, OK 74401 (918) 686-6624

West Bottoms Stockyards
1600 Genessee Street
Kansas City, MO 64102

Resources on the Chisholm Trail
(alphabetical)

Abilene Visitors Center
Free admission, free parking
http://www.abilenekansas.org
201 Nw 2nd St. Abilene, KS (785) 263-2550

Belton County Museum
Free admission, free parking
http://www.bellcountytx.com/Museum
201 N. Main, Belton, TX 76513 (254)933-5243

Bob Bullock Museum
Admission charged, parking fees
http://www.thestoryoftexas.com
1800 Congress Ave, Austin, TX 78711 (512) 936-8746

Caldwell County Museum
Admission charge, free parking
http://www.lockhart-tx.org
314 E Market St, Lockhart, TX 78644

Canadian County Museum
Admission charged, free parking
http://www.elreno.org/tour/attractions.asp
300 South Grand Avenue El Reno, OK 73036 (405) 262-5121

Chisholm Trail Heritage Center
Admission charged, free parking
http://www.onthechisholmtrail.com/
1000 Chisholm Trail Parkway Duncan, OK 73533 (405) 262-5121

Chisholm Trail Heritage Museum
(currently under restoration)
http://www.chisholmtrailmuseum.org
(361)277-2866

Chisholm Trail Museum (Kingfisher, Oklahoma)
Admission charged, free parking
605 Zellers Avenue Kingfisher, OK 73750-4228 (405)375-5176

Chisholm Trail Museum (Waurika, Oklahoma)
Free Admission, free parking
http://www.waurika.net/museum.html
Intersection US 81 and US 70 in Waurika, OK 73573

Denton County Courthouse-on-the-Square Museum
Free admission, parking fees may apply
http://dentoncounty.com
110 West Hickory Denton, TX 76201 (940)349-2850

Dwight D. Eisenhower Presidential Library
Admission charged, free parking
http://www.eisenhower.utexas.edu
200 S.E. 4th Street Abilene, KS 67410 (785) 263-6700

Fort Worth Stockyards National Historic District
Free admission to stockyards, museum fees vary; parking fees
http://www.fortworthstockyards.org
North Main and Exchange Avenue, Fort Worth, TX

Grapevine Vintage Railroad
Admission charged, free parking
https://www.grapevinetexasusa.com
Stockyards Station in Fort Worth Stockyards or 706 Main Street, Grapevine, TX 76051
(817) 410-8136

Great Plains Transportation Museum
Admission charged, free parking, open seasonally
http://www.gptm.us
700 East Douglas Wichita, Kansas 67202 (316) 263-0944

Harvey County Historical Society Museum and Archives
Admission charged, free parking
http://www.hchm.org/index.html
203 N Main Newton, KS 67114 (316) 283-2221

Historic Fort Reno
Admission charged, free parking
http://www.fortreno.org
7107 W. Cheyenne St. El Reno, OK 73036 (405)262-3987

Kansas Aviation Museum
Admission charged, free parking
http://kansasaviationmuseum.org
3350 South George Washington Blvd. Wichita, KS 67210 (316) 683-9242

Kauffman Museum
Admission charged, free parking
http://www.bethelks.edu/kauffman/
27th and North Main, Bethel College, North Newton, KS 67117 (316) 283-1612

Layland Museum
Free admission, free parking
http://www.ci.cleburne.tx.us/museum.aspx
201 N. Caddo Cleburne, TX 76033 (817)556-8840

Mayborn Museum Complex at Baylor University
Admission charged, parking fees may apply
http://www.baylor.edu/mayborn
1300 S. University Parks Waco, TX 76706 (254)710-1110

Morton Museum
Advanced notification, admission charged, free parking
http://www.mortonmuseum.org
210 S Dixon St. Gainesville, TX 76241 (940)668-8900

Old Cowtown Museum
Admission charged, free parking
http://www.oldcowtown.org
1871 Sim Park Drive Wichita, KS 67203 (316) 219-1871

Old Town Marketplace
Free admission, museum fees vary; free parking
http://www.oldtownwichita.com
East Douglas Avenue between North Broadway and North Washington Streets in Wichita, KS

Railroad Museum of Oklahoma
Admission charged, free parking
http://railroadmuseumofoklahoma.org
702 N Washington, Enid OK 73701 (580)233-3051

Round Rock Visitors Center
Free admission, free parking
http://www.sportscapitaloftexas.com
212 Main Street, Round Rock, TX 78664 (512)218-7023

Salado Visitor's Guide
http://www.salado-tx.com

Sedgwick County Museum
Admission charged, parking fees
http://www.wichitahistory.org
204 S. Main Wichita, KS 67202 (316) 265-9314

Tails 'n Trails Museum
Admission charged, free parking
http://talesntrails.org
1522 E. Highway 82, Nocona, TX 76255 (940) 825-5330

Texas Ranger Museum
Admission charged, free parking
http://www.texasranger.org
100 Texas Ranger Trail Waco, TX 76706 (254)750-8631

Thistle Hill
Advanced booking, admission charged, free parking
http://www.historicfortworth.org
1509 Pennsylvania Avenue Fort Worth, TX 76104 (817) 332-5875

Wichita Art Museum
Admission charged, parking fees may apply
http://wichitaartmuseum.org
1400 West Museum Boulevard Wichita, KS 67203 (316) 268-4921

Williamson County Museum
Free admission, free parking
http://www.williamsonmuseum.org
716 S. Austin Avenue, Georgetown, TX 78626 (512)943-1670

Wise County Museum
Admission charged, free parking
http://www.wisehistory.com
1602 S Trinity St. Decatur, TX 76234 (940)627-5586

Old Town Abilene
Free admission, museum and train fees vary; free parking
http://www.abilenekansas.org
100 SE 5th Street Abilene, KS 67410 (785)263-1868

Resources on the Great Western Trail (alphabetical)

Boot Hill Museum
Admission charged, free parking
http://boothill.org
Front Street Dodge City, KS 67801(620)227-8188

Buffalo Gap Historic Village
Admission charged, free parking
http://www.buffalogap.com
133 N. William Street Buffalo Gap, TX 79508 (325)572-3365

Camp Verde General Store
Free Admission, free parking
http://www.campverdegeneralstore.com
285 Camp Verde Road East Camp Verde, TX 78010 (830)634-7722

Dalton Gange Hideout (Meade Historical Society)
Admission charged, free parking
http://www.oldmeadecounty.com/hideout.htm
Meade, KS 67864 (620)873-2731 or (800)354-2743

Dodge City Visitors Center
Free admission, free parking
http://www.visitdodgecity.org
400 W. Wyatt Earp Boulevard Dodge City, KS 67801 (620)225-8186 or (800) OLD-WEST

Elk City Old Town Museum Complex
Admission charged, free parking
http://www.elkcity.com
U.S. 66 and Pioneer Road Elk City, OK 73648 (580)225-6266

Fort Dodge (now Kansas Soldiers Retirement Home)
Free admission, free parking
http://www.forttours.com/pages/fortdodge.asp
400 East Highway Fort Dodge, KS 67801 (620) 227-2121

Fort Griffin State Historic Site
Admission charged, free parking
http://www.visitfortgriffin.com
1701 N. US Hwy 283 Albany, TX 76430 (325)762-3592

Fort Supply State Historic Site
Admission charged, free parking
http://www.okhistory.org/outreach/military/fortsupply.html
US 183/270/412 and OK 3 in Fort Supply, OK (580)766-3767

Frontier Museum
Admission charged, free parking
http://www.frontiertimesmuseum.org/
510 13th St Bandera, TX 78003 (830) 796-3864

Frontier! Texas
Admission charged, free parking
http://www.frontiertexas.com
625 North First Street Abilene, TX 79601 (325)437-2800

Heart of Texas Museum
Admission charged, free parking
http://www.heartoftexashistoricalmuseum.com
117 North High Street Brady, TX 76825 (325)597-0526

Mason Square Museum
Admission charged, free parking
http://www.masonsquaremuseum.org
103 Fort MacKavitt Mason, TX 76856 (325)347-0507

Museum of the Western Prairie
Opening in 2011
http://www.okhistory.org/outreach/museums/westernprairie.html
1100 Memorial Drive Altus, OK 73521 (580)482-1044

Old Jail Art Center
Admission charged, free parking
http://www.theoldjailartcenter.org
201 S 2nd, Albany, TX 76430 (325)762-2269

Plains Indians and Pioneer Museum
Admission charged, free parking
http://www.pipm1.org
2009 Williams Avenue Woodward, OK 73801 (580)256 6136

Red River Valley Museum
Admission charged, free parking
http://www.redrivervalleymuseum.org
4600 College Drive Vernon, TX 76384 (940)553-1848

San Antonio Missions National Historic Park
Free admission, free parking (except at the Alamo)
http://www.nps.gov/saan/index.htm
Begin at the Alamo. Obtain map at Visitor Center to locate the other missions.
300 Alamo Plaza San Antonio, TX 78205

Bibliography

49th Congress, Second Session, House of Representatives, Ex.Doc No. 267. Letter from the Secretary of Treasury, March 2 1885.

Anbinder, Tyler. *Five Points: The Nineteenth-Century New York City Neighborhood ThatInvented Tap Dance, Stole Elections and Became the Worlds Most Notorious Slum.* New York: Free Press, 2001.

Calloway, Colin G. (Editor). *Our Hearts Fell to the Ground: Plains Indians Views of How the West was Lost.* Boston: Bedford/ St. Martin's Press, 1996.

Dykstra, Robert. "The Cattle Towns Adjust to Violence (with a Postscript)." *Major Problems in the History of the American West*, 2nd edition, edited by Clyde Milner, et al. Boston: Houghton Mifflin Company, 1997.

Enid Justin Oral History, the University of North Texas Libraries and Archives.

Galenson, David . "The End of the Chisholm Trail." *The Journal of Economic History* 34, no. 2 (June 1974).

Goodnight, Charles. *Land: Beales Grant and Documentation*, 1882-1889 and undated. Center for American History, the University of Texas at Austin.

Guice, John D. Guice "The Cattle Raisers of the Old Southwest: a Reinterpretation." *The Western Historical Quarterly* 8 n. 2 (April 1977).

Hunter, Marvin J. (Editory) *The Trail Drivers of Texas* [1925]. Austin: University of Texas Press, 1985.

John Hamilton Baker Diaries, 1861-1918. Center for American History, the University of Texas at Austin.

Jordan, Terry G. Jordan. "The Origin of Anglo-American Cattle Ranching in Texas: Documentation of Diffusion from the Lower South." *Economic Geography* 45, no. 1 (January, 1969).

Limerick, Patricia Nelson. *The Legacy of Conquest: The Unbroken Past of the American West.* New York: W.W. Norton and Company, 1987.

McCoy, Joseph McCoy. *Historic Sketches of the Cattle Trade of the West and Southwest by Joseph McCoy, the pioneer Western Cattle Shipper* Kansas City: Ramsey, Millet, and Hudson, 1874.

Ridings, Sam P. *The Chisholm Trail: A History of the World's Greatest Cattle Trail* Guthrie, Oklahoma: Co-Operative Publishing Company, 1936.

Tennant, H.S. "The Texas Cattle Trails." *Chronicles of Oklahoma* 14 no. 1 (March 1936).

Texas Longhorn Breeders of America Association, http://www.tlbaa.org/Resources/lhhistory.html.

Texas Ordinance of Secession: A Declaration of the Causes which Impel the State of Texas to Secede from the Federal Union, 1861. Texas State Library and Archives, Austin.

Webb, Walter Prescott. *The Great Plains: A compelling History of the Great Central Plains and how this Land has shaped the Destiny of the American Nation.* New York: Grosset and Dunlap, 1931.

White, Christine Schulz and Benton R. *Now the Wolf Has Come: The Creek Nation in the Civil War.* College Station: Texas A&M University Press, 1996).

Index

98th Meridian 85,98,99,104,112 (178)
Abilene, Kansas 12,22,68,70,91,109,110,115,116,117,158,159,162
Abilene, Texas 7,120,130,131,132,163
Addington, Oklahoma 6,8,67,98,101,102
Alamo, The (San Antonio, Texas) 120,121,122,164
Albany, Texas 120,131,132,163
Altus, Oklahoma 135,136,137,138,163
Arapahos 20,106,119,135,143
Arkansas River 55,112,150
Ashland, Kansas 145,147,148
Atoka, Oklahoma 42,48,49,155
Austin, Stephen F. 124
Austin, Texas 24,31,71,72,73,74,158
Baker, Jonathan Hamilton 21
Baird, Texas 120,130,132
Bandera, Texas 120,123,124,163
Bandera Pass 123
Barbed wire 8,17,24,79,179
Barrow, Clyde 49
Bass, Sam 74,75,83,94
Baxter Springs, Kansas 6,58,59,60,61,155
Belton, Texas 71,77,78,158
Big and Little Basins 8,118,145,146,148,149
Big Nose Kate 22
Big Thicket 14
Black Beaver 68,100
Black Kettle 140,143
Black Kettle National Grasslands 140
Blizzards 18,98,112
Blunt, James 39
Boggy Creek 59
Boggy Depot, Oklahoma 6,30,42,46,47,48,155
Bolivar, Texas 92,94,95
Boot Hill (cemetery) 21,110,111,149,151,162
Bowie, James (Jim) 121
Bowie, Texas 71,86,87
Brady, Texas 120,128,129,163
Brazos River 7,12,73,78,79,80,81,132,133
Brothels 7,22,59,63,84,89,93,112,150
Brown, Joshua D. 124
Brownwood, Texas 130
Bryan, John Neeley 31,32,45
Buffalo 10,20,21,29,31,32,90,91,98,119,131,142,145,146,147,148,150
Buffalo Gap, Texas 120,130,131,162
Buffalo Soldiers 104

Buffalo (Springs), Oklahoma 135,144,145
Butch Cassidy and the Sundance Kid 83
Butler, Oklahoma 135,140,141
Butterfield-Overland Stage Coach Company 37,38,47,48,87,94,97,131
Caddos 89,126
Caldwell, Kansas 12,21,109,110,111
California Trail 46,50,87,96,133
Camino Real de los Tejas 73
Camp Verde, Texas 123,124,162
Canute, Oklahoma 135,140,180
Carmago, Oklahoma 135,141,142
Carpenter's Bluff, Texas 40
Cedar Springs, Texas 32,142
Celina, Texas 31,35
Checotah, Oklahoma 42,53,54,156
Cherokees 43,52,53,55,56,78,108
Cherokee Strip Livestock Association 24
Cheyennes 10,20,107,119,135,143
Chicago, Illinois 14,21,30 (176)
Chicago and Rock Island Railroad 25,104
Chickasaws 43,44,45,47,48,55,70,98,99,103
Chickasha, Oklahoma 98,103,104
Chisholm, Jesse 7,68,102,105,106,107
Chisholm, Thornton 70,71,72
Chisum, John 17,70,94,95
Choctaws 43,44,46,47,48,51,55,70,103
Cleburne, Texas 71,81,160
Colbert, Benjamin 38,44,45
Colbert, Oklahoma 42,43,44
Coleman, Robert 130
Coleman, Texas 46,120,129,130
Colorado River 73,74
Chuck wagon 6,17
Cimarron River 8,146,147
Civilian Conservation Corps 51
Civil War 10,14,15,16,17,23,29,32,34,39,43,45,48,50,53,54,57,59,60,61,65,68,69, 72,73,76,77,79,82,87,96,112,119, 122, 123, 124, 128,166
Coffee, Holland 29,38,39,40
Comanches 10,56,88,89,96,103,119,126,128,129,133,135
Cowboys 7,12,15,16,17,18,19,20,21,22,24,25,26,27,29,30,31,32,38,60,70,73,79, 80,83,89,90,91,95,98,101,109,110, 118,124,128,136,146,153,154
Cowboys, African American 7,16,18,54,101
Cross Timbers 19,21,85,98
Custer, General Armstrong 140, 143
Dakotas (territories) 10,24,25,119
Dawes Commission 55
Dallas, Texas 6,21,31,32,33,53,155

168

Davis, Jefferson 124
Dead Line, The 149,150
Deep Hole Crossing, Oklahoma 145,146,147
Denton, Texas 17,70,85,92,93,94,159
Denison, Texas 23,31,34,37,38,39,40,41,42,43,70,156,157
Doan's Crossing, Texas 44,120,134,135,136
Doby Springs, Oklahoma 135,144,145
Doc Holliday 22
Dodge City, Kansas 8,12,21,22,23,118,145,146,147,149,150,151,162,163
Dorchester, Texas 6,31,36,37
Dougherty, James M. 68
Dover, Oklahoma 98
Driskill, Jesse 74
Duncan, Oklahoma 98,102,158
Durant, Dixon 44
Durant, Oklahoma 42,44,45,155,157
Edwardsville, Oklahoma 135,140
Eisenhower, Dwight D. 40,41,43,33,115,159
Elk City, Oklahoma 135,139,140,162
Elizabethtown, Texas 92,93
Ellsworth, Kansas 12,21,22,70,110,116
El Reno, Oklahoma 98,104,105,106,158,160
Englewood, Kansas 149
Enid, Oklahoma 27,98,107,108,161
Fargo, Oklahoma 134,135,142,143,169
Farmers 16,17,23,24,30,43,47,60,68,70,95,123,145
Federal Writer's Project 26,144,154
Five Civilized Tribes 15,20,42,55,135
Five Points, New York 14
Fleetwood, Oklahoma 7,98,99,100
Floods (flashfloods, freshets) 63,98,125,147
Ford, Robert 66
Fort Arbuckle, Oklahoma 50,103
Fort Blunt, Oklahoma 57
Fort Dodge, Kansas 150,151,162,163
Fort Gibson, Oklahoma 6,30,42,55,56,57,58,155
Fort Griffin State Historical Park, Texas 120,132,133,163
Fort Griffin Flat, Texas 7,22,132
Fort Mason, Texas 128
Fort McKavett, Texas 127
Fort Phantom Hill, Texas 7,117,130,131
Fort Reno, Oklahoma 160
Fort Sill, Oklahoma 20,103,107
Fort Supply, Oklahoma 8,135,143,144,163,119,142
Fort Washita, Oklahoma 6,29,42,45,46,50,155
Fort Worth, Texas 6,7,8,13,21,22,23,26,71,81,82,83,84,85,92,159,161
Foss, Oklahoma 135,140

Friendship, Oklahoma 135,137,138
Frisco, Texas 31,34,35,36,155
Gainesville, Texas 19,92,95,96,160
Galveston, Texas 31
Geary, Oklahoma 48,98,105,106
Georgetown, Texas 71,76,161
Giesecke, Walter 21
Glidden, Joseph 24
Goodnight, Charles 17,119,133
Goodnight-Loving Trail 129
Grandpappy's Point, Texas 31,40
Great Depression 26,37,101,136,151
Green Corn Rebellion 43
Granite, Oklahoma 135,137,138
Gulf, Colorado and Santa Fe Railroad 25
Gunter, Texas 31,35,36
Hamilton, Raymond 49
Hannibal and St. Joseph Railroad 68
Harper, Texas 120,124,125
Headquarters Mountains, Oklahoma 138
Hell's Half Acre (Fort Worth, Texas) 21,81,83
Hennessey, Oklahoma 97,107,108
Hersey, Tim 68,69,71
Hickock, Wild Bill 23
Honey Springs, Oklahoma 54,56
Hord's Creek, Texas 130
Horton, F.M. 20,119
Houston, Sam 38,78,130
Hunter, J. Marvin 26,153,165
Illinois 14,16,68
Illinois Bend 90
Indian Bureau 55
Indian Removal Act (1830) 56
Indian Territory 12,14,15,16,17,20,24,25,30,42,43,48,50,53,54,55,56,59,68,69,
70,78,87,89,95,98,99,106,109,118,119,128,136,145,147,154
James, Frank 51
James, Jesse 51,53,60,64,65,66,156
Jefferson, Oklahoma 98,109
Jefferson, Thomas 147
Justin, Enid 165
Justin, H.J. 70,87,89
Justin, Texas 93
Kansas City, Missouri 6,14,30,58,60,61,62,63,64,65,116,156,158
Kansas River 6,62
Kerr, James 124
Kerrville, Texas 120,123,124
Kiamichi Mountains 48

Kimball, Texas 71,80,81
Kingfisher, Oklahoma 98,106,107,159
Kiowa, Oklahoma 42,48,49
Kiowas 8,10,96,103,119,128,135,143
Klemme, Bob 27
Kremlin, Oklahoma 98,108,109
Lake Altus 136
Lake Texoma 38,39,40,44
Lakotas 10
Lattimore, Tom 7,101
Laverne, Oklahoma 135,144
Leedey, Oklahoma 8,135,141
Lehigh, Kansas 7,109,114,115
Lipans 128
Llano Estacado , Texas 17
Llano River 7,125
Lockhart, Texas 71,72,73,158
Lone Wolf, Oklahoma 7,135,137,138
London, Texas 7,120,124,125,126
Longhorn cattle 12,14,15,17,23,24,29,30,31,32,69,84,90,102,123,146,166
Louisiana 65,72,73
Louisiana Purchase 147
Loving, Oliver 17
Lytle, John 17,118,134
Marcy, Randalph B. 37,50,86,96,133
Marlow, Oklahoma 98,102,103
Mason, Texas 126,128,163
Masterson, Bat 23
May, Oklahoma 135,144
McAlester, Oklahoma 42,48,49,50,51,156
McCoy, Joseph 16,23,41,68,69,70,72,115
McCoy, John Calvin 62
McCulloch, Hugh 24,25
Meade, Oklahoma 149,162
Medford, Oklahoma 98.109,110
Medina River 123
Menard, Texas 7,120,126,127,128
Meridian, Texas 71,80
Mexican-American War 45
Mexico 6,15,17,73,121,122
Meyers, Colonel J.J. 71
Minneola, Kansas 145,149
Missouri-Kansas-Texas Railroad (M-K-T or KATY) 6, 25,37,38,40,41,42,44,61,157
Missouri-Oklahoma-Gulf Railroad 41
Missouri River 21,25,37,41,42,48,49,50,54,55,61,77,142
Montague, Texas 71,87,88

171

Montana 24,119
Monument Hill 6,7,8,67,101,102
Muskogee, Oklahoma 42,54,55,56,58,155,157
National Cattle Road 25
National Park Service 27
Nebraska 25,60
New Mexico 70,95,129,151,17
New Orleans 14,31
Newton, Kansas 109,113,114,159,160
New York City 14
Nocona, Texas 71,87,88,90,91,92,97,133
Oklahoma Land Rush 24,108,109,137,139,140,143
Old Retrop, Oklahoma 8,135,138,139
Oregon Trail 62
Ozark Mountains 59
Palo Duro Canyon 37
Palo Pinto, Texas 21
Parilla, Captain Diego Ortiz 88,89,127
Perryville, Oklahoma 49,50
Peta Nocona 133
Pike, Zebulon 147
Pittsburg, Oklahoma 6,42,48,49
Plains Indians 16,20,21,46,56,98,100,119,135,142,143,145,164
Plano, Texas 31,33,34,35,156,157
Pond Creek, Oklahoma 98,109
Pony Express 6,60,64,65,66,157
Port, Oklahoma 135,138,139
Porum, Oklahoma 42,52,54
Porter, James 39
Pottsboro, Texas 31,38,40
Preston (Bend), Texas 6,29,31,38,39
Preston Trail or Preston Road 32,33,34,35,36,37,38,40
Prosper, Texas 31,35
Quachita Forest 53
Quantrill's Guerillas (Raiders) 39,53,59
Quantrill, William 59
Quartz Mountains State Park 137,138
Ranchers 10,14,17,24,41,43,47,128,133
Rayburn, Sam 38
Reconstruction Treaties (1866) 16
Red Fork Station, Oklahoma 98,107
Red River 7,12,16,19,33,37,38,39,40,41,43,44,86,87,88,89,90,96,98,134,135
Red River Station, Texas 71,87,90,91,98,99
Red River Wars 16
Reed, Jim 53
Remuda 18
Retrop, Oklahoma 135,138,139

Rientesville, Oklahoma 42,53,54
Ringgold, Texas 71,92,97
Rio Grande Valley 12,31
Roanoke, Texas 92,93
Robbers Cave State Park 51,52,157
Robidoux, Joseph 65
Rock Crossing (Bluff) 40
Rock Island Railroad (Chicago and Rock Island Railroad) 100,102,104,106,116
Rogers, Will 43
Roosevelt, Franklin D.26,27
Roosevelt, Eleanor 94
Round Rock, Texasc6,31,71,74,75,76,161
Route 66 58,59,60,104,105,106,139,140
Running Buffalo 20,119
Rush Springs, Oklahoma 98,103
Ryan, Oklahoma 98,100
Salado, Texas 71,76,77,161
Saloons 7,22,59,63,69,83,89,111,112,123,146,150
San Antonio, Texas 7,31,73,120,121,122,164
Santa Anna, Texas 120,121,129
San Saba Presidio and Mission 88,126,127
Santa Fe Trail 62,149,150,151
Saunders, George 26
Sedalia, Missouri 30,58,60,61,92,68,157
Seymour, Texas 120,133,134
Sherman, Texas 31,37,38,39,40,156
Shreveport, Louisiana 14
Sioux 10
Sivell's Bend, Texas 92,96,97
Smoky Hill River 116
Spanish Fort, Texas 7,22,70,71,87,88,89,90,97,127
Starr, Belle 52,53,54
Starr, Sam 51,53
St. Jacob's Well 145,148
St. Jo, Texas 7,92,97
St. Joseph, Missouri 30,58,60,62,64,65,66,70,72,156,157
St. Louis and San Francisco Railway (Frisco) 25
St. Louis, Missouri 14,21,25,30,31,34,41,43,61,65,151
St. Louis and Southwestern Railway (Cotton Belt) 37
Stockyards 6,7,12,13,30, 60,62,63,64,65,70,81,83,84,85,92,122,158,159
Stokes Commission 56
Stringtown, Oklahoma 42,48,49
Suttenfield, Sophia 38,39
Sweazy, Carl 119
Taylor, Zachary 45
Taovayans 88,89
Taovaya Bridge 90

Terral, Oklahoma 92,99,100
Texas and Pacific Railroad 93,131,132
Texas Fever 23,30
Texas Rangers 24,77,79
Throckmorton, Texas 120,133
Tornado Alley 18,98
Tornadoes (twisters) 18,98
Trail of Tears 42,43,56
Trail, Oklahoma 141,142
Trinity River 31,32,33,82,84,97
Union Pacific Railroad 48,115
Vernon, Texas 120,133,134,164
Vici, Oklahoma 135,141,142
Waco, Texas 6,31,34,71,77,78,79,80,160
Wacos 78
Waggoner-Wharton, Electra 84
Waggoners (ranch and mansion) 85,134
Warren, Oklahooma 135,137,138
Washington, D.C. 24
Waurika, Oklahoma 98,100,101,159
Weather 18,32,98,125
Wellington, Kansas 109,111
Wells, Ida Barnett 43
West Bottoms (Kansas City) 60,62,63,64,158
Wheeler, Colonel O. 69
Wichita Falls, Texas 96
Wichita Falls and Northwestern Railway 144
Wichita, Kansas 23,109,111,112,113,159,160,161
Wichita Mountains 118,136,167
Wichitas 10,69,78,88,89,103
Woodward, Oklahoma 135,142,143,164
Works Progress Administration 26,57,94,154
Wranglers 18
Wyoming 24,119
Yates, Texas 120,124,125
Yelton, Oklahoma 135,144,145

Shameless Self Promotional Page

For the Road Tripper who doesn't have everything just yet...
Check out the other titles in the Traveling History Series!

Traveling History Up the Cattle Trails:
A Road Tripper's Guide to the Cattle Roads of the Southwest

Traveling History Amongst the Ghosts:
A Road Tripper's Guide to Ghost Towns in the Red River Valley

Traveling History Along the Rails:
A Road Tripper's Guide to Railroads of the Red River Valley

Traveling History With Bonnie and Clyde:
A Road Tripper's Guide to Gangster Sites in Middle America

Come join the great people who make their vacations into adventurous, fun, and informative road trips!

Contact
Red River Historian Press
Robin Cole Jett
214-404-3459
robin@RedRiverHistorian.com

To book presentations and order the Traveling History Guides, or just to discover more stories, photos, and fun stuff, visit:
http://www.RedRiverHistorian.com

[1] Tyler Anbinder, *Five Points: The Nineteenth-Century New York City Neighborhood That Invented Tap Dance, Stole Elections and Became the Worlds Most Notorious Slum* (New York: Free Press, 2001), 14.
[2] 49th Congress, Second Session, House of Representatives, Ex.Doc No. 267. Letter from the Secretary of Treasury, March 2 1885, 12-35.
[3] The great packing houses got their start after the Civil War. Phillip Armour and Gustavo Swift both set up shop in 1867 to capitalize on the large amounts of Texas cattle that were being driven north to Chicago.
[4] Patricia Nelson Limerick, *The Legacy of Conquest: The Unbroken Past of the American West* (New York: W.W. Norton and Company, 1987), 27.
[5] The Cherokees, Choctaws, Chickasaws, Creeks, and Seminoles comprised the so-called Five Civilized Tribes, who were forcibly removed to Indian Territory from their southeastern U.S. homelands during the 1820s. These tribes each formed their own "domestic dependent nation," with a constitution, active government, and sets of laws. The Southern Plains tribes consisted of the Comanches, Kiowas, Cheyennes, Apaches, and Wichitas (with related subgroups).
[6] The Creeks under Opotehleyahola fled Indian Territory to escape the vindictiveness of their brethren, the McIntosh Creeks. They camped at Fort Leavenworth, where, due to the lack of shelter and blankets, over two thousand died during a long, cold winter. Christine Schulz White and Benton R. White, *Now the Wolf Has Come: The Creek Nation in the Civil War* (College Station: Texas A&M University Press, 1996).
[7] Texas Longhorn Breeders of America Association, http://www.tlbaa.org/Resources/lhhistory.html. Accessed 29 December 2009, 21.21 CST.
[8] Cattle handling methods developed independently from each other in various regions of the New World, as immigrants brought their own customs to animal husbandry. Evidence from the earliest American cattle handling methods, with Anglo-influenced ways, can be found in North Carolina, whereas Latin American, South American, Texan, and Floridian cowboys employed Spanish methods. See Terry G. Jordan, "The Origin of Anglo-American Cattle Ranching in Texas: a Documentation of Diffusion from the Lower South." *Economic Geography* 45, no. 1 (January, 1969); John D. Guice, "The Cattle Raisers of the Old Southwest: a Reinterpretation." *The Western Historical Quarterly* 8 n. 2 (April 1977).
[9] Marvin J. Hunter, *The Trail Drivers of Texas* [1925] (Austin: University of Texas Press, 1985), 223.
[10] Ibid, 392-393.
[11] John Hamilton Baker Diaries, 1861-1918. Center for American History, the University of Texas at Austin.
[12] Enid Justin Oral History, the University of North Texas Libraries and Archives.

[13] Robert Dykstra. "The Cattle Towns Adjust to Violence (with a Postscript)." *Major Problems in the History of the American West*, 2nd edition, edited by Clyde Milner, et al (Boston: Houghton Mifflin Company, 1997), 206-221.
[14] Joseph McCoy, *Historic Sketches of the Cattle Trade of the West and Southwest by Joseph McCoy, the pioneer Western Cattle Shipper* (Kansas City: Ramsey, Millet, and Hudson, 1874).
[15] David Galenson, "The End of the Chisholm Trail." *The Journal of Economic History* 34, no. 2 (June 1974).
[16] 49th Congress, 2nd Session. House of Representatives, ex. Doc. No. 267. Letter from the Secretary of the Treasury, March 1885.
[17] In Indian Territory, Kansas, and Missouri, the Shawnee Trail was also known as the Texas Trail in reference to the many Texas-bound pioneers. U.S. Army commanders in the Southwest simply called it a "military road." The moniker "Preston Road" was used in North Texas. Coincidentally, Preston Road still runs from Dallas north to the Red River.
[18] A calaboose is a free-standing, one-room jail cell built of concrete, usually set just behind the town's center. Calabooses proliferated in small towns throughout the southwest. Their purpose was to detain alleged criminals before they could be transported to the county jails. Most of the time, these jails held the town drunk, hence its nickname, "the drunk tank." The term "calaboose" originates from the Spanish *calabozo*, meaning "dungeon."
[19] Denison, Texas, was home to Thomas Munson, a world-famous viticulturalist whose hybrid strand of grapes saved the French wine industry in the late 19th century.
[20] Oklahoma tenant farmers joined the Socialist Party in record numbers during the early 20th century as a response to land speculation, fraud, and abuse by wealthy landowners, railroads, businessmen, bankers, and local governments. The farmers eventually unionized into the Working Class Union (WCU), which looked for more of a collectivist approach to agriculture. The WCU farmers greatly opposed the state-mandated dipping of their cattle to ward against "Texas Fever," a tick-borne disease, believing the dipping to be more deadly than the fever. They also opposed the 1917 Conscription Act. White, black, and Indian farmers banded together to oppose the draft in what was called the "Green Corn Rebellion," so named because the participants roasted green corn on their way to protest the draft in Washington, D.C. Oklahoma militias and posses halted their movements, and the resulting clashes left three men dead. Thereafter, the movement lost steam, especially as many powerful Oklahomans did their best to oust the Socialist Party – and subsequent agrarian reforms - from their state.
[21] Much of Colbert's ferry business, which began in the 1850s, was supplanted by the railroad, but Colbert did not retire from ferrying. Instead, he built a toll bridge east of the KATY bridge. He later became an executive in the Red River Toll Bridge Company after they bought out his toll bridge charter. The building of a free bridge (US 75) in the 1930s caused the Red River Toll

Bridge Company to win an injunction against the free bridge's use. This angered Oklahoma's governor, "Alfalfa Bill" Murray, who ended up destroying the Oklahoma approach to the toll bridge to force the use of the free bridge. The "Red River Bridge War" finally came to a halt when the Red River Toll Bridge Company was paid out for the remainder of its contract, and the free bridge was put into permanent use.

[22] Just north of Narcissa is an original stretch of the Route 66 ribbon road. To follow it, turn right (east) onto ED 140. You can follow the ribbon road all the way into Miami. It will merge with OK 125 and enter town by the fairgrounds. Continue north to meet up with US 69/ OK 66 in downtown Miami.

[23] McCoy, chapter 2.

[24] The term "carpetbagger" has been used since the end of the Civil War to identify northerners who came to do business in the South. Though it has a derogatory meaning – southern whites viewed these businessmen as a "second invasion" of sorts – in reality, the northern influx of money and ideas helped to spawn what historians have termed the New South, with economies based on trade, manufacturing, and transportation.

[25] Some folklorists maintain that Joseph McCoy's fulfilled promise to the cattle drivers became the origination of the phrase, "the Real McCoy." However, other versions state that the term authenticates good liquor, such as rum that was run by English privateer Bill McCoy in the 18th century. Elijah McCoy, the inventor of a reliable system of lubricating steam locomotives, is also considered an original source.

[26] Historians have argued over the naming of the trails since the early 1930s, when trail drivers came together at reunions to record the history of their undertakings. Trail drivers really didn't care what the names were – they'd use Chisholm, Western, or Eastern trail interchangeably (especially because the Chisholm was Eastern to the Western, but Western to the Shawnee Trail, confusing everybody.) By the 1940s, when the Federal Writer's Project created its western history collection, the designation "Chisholm Trail" had come into wide use, so the name stuck, even if the trail, as forged by Jesse Chisholm, never extended into Texas.

[27] Today, the Swedes have come to Round Rock yet again – this time, in the form of an IKEA store.

[28] Waco's black business district on Elm Street was once home to a vibrant neighborhood. Paul Quinn College, the first private African American college in Texas, was established here in 1882. However, a large number of African Americans fled the city after the violent lynching of Jesse Washington, a mentally handicapped young man who was roasted alive in downtown Waco in 1916.

[29] In his seminal regional study, *The Great Plains* (1931), Historian Walter Prescott Webb argued that large scale agriculture was not sustainable west of the 98th Meridian, and most land could only be used for cattle grazing. See

Walter Prescott Webb, *The Great Plains: A compelling History of the Great Central Plains and how this Land has shaped the Destiny of the American Nation* (New York: Grosset and Dunlap, 1931).

[30] The Waggoners made their first fortune driving cattle up the Chisholm Trail, then began leasing grazing land from the federal government and Indian reservations in Oklahoma Territory. With the advent of barbed wire, the Waggoners began buying up little farms and ranches all around them (and at times undercutting them to force them into bankruptcy, then snatching up the land at bargain prices). In its prime, the Waggoner Ranch comprised over a million acres. Today, the Waggoner Ranch, with its headquarters in Vernon, has been incorporated and still holds vast swaths of land from Wise County all the way into Wichita Falls and beyond.

[31] These types of raids have been historically called 'depredations,' but that term discounts Southern Plains Indians' cultures. Nomadic tribes such as the Comanches, Kiowas, Cheyennes, and Apaches stole horses from settlers and missions to count towards "coup," or war bounties. The more coup a warrior took, the more esteem he garnered. Obtaining horses was also a way of asserting his authority over what had historically been his territory. While settlers accused the Native Americans of stealing, the idea of privately held property in an era of open range was a foreign concept to the natives. The settlers seemed to have understood this, at least in some instances. Whereas an American horse thief would be hanged in accordance to frontier justice, often settlers either just took back the horses, or negotiated for their return. When a fight did ensue over the livestock, the parties engaged in real battles, marking a distinct range and culture war.

[32] Historians have argued that Parilla's failed attempt at overtaking the post in what is today Spanish Fort accounts for the lack of Spanish colonial influence in North Texas.

[33] The lands of the Indian nations extended all the way from east to west across Indian Territory before 1865. After the Civil War, the United States renegotiated treaties with the nations. Indian Territory was divided up further, making room not only for other ousted tribes, but also for the railroad. The 1866 treaties would eventually lead to the loss of nation status for the tribes, the creation of Oklahoma Territory, the Sooner Land Rushes, and the Dawes Commission.

[34] Pizza Hut and White Castle, among others, originated in Wichita.

[35] H.S. Tennant, "The Texas Cattle Trails." *Chronicles of Oklahoma* 14 no. 1 (March 1936), 84. The historic run of the Great Western Trail was rediscovered in the 1930s with the Federal Writer's Project of the Works Progress Administration, and most of the trail's historic path was related in Tennant's article, using first-person accounts and plenty of back roads exploration.

[36] Sam P. Ridings, *The Chisholm Trail: A History of the World's Greatest Cattle Trail* (Guthrie, Oklahoma: Co-Operative Publishing Company, 1936): 179-180.

[37] Sam P. Ridings explained that "wohaw," a pan-Indian word for "cattle," may have derived from commands given to oxen by their pioneer drivers.

[38] Carl Sweezy, "Learning the White Man's Ways." Excerpted from *Our Hearts Fell to the Ground: Plains Indians Views of How the West was Lost*, edited by Colin G. Calloway (Boston: Bedford/ St. Martin's Press, 1996): 165-166.

[39] Texas Ordinance of Secession: A Declaration of the Causes which Impel the State of Texas to Secede from the Federal Union, 1861. Texas State Library and Archives, Austin.

[40] Charles Goodnight, *Land: Beales Grant and Documentation*, 1882-1889 and undated. Center for American History, the University of Texas at Austin. The Pease River Battle was significant for another reason: Cynthia Ann Parker, a white woman who was kidnapped as a child at her family's fort near Mexia, Texas and became Comanche Chief Peta Nocona's wife, was discovered by the American fighters after the battle was over and Peta Nocona was killed. Because Cynthia Ann knew no other life but the Comanche ways, she resented her forced re-entry into white society for the rest of her short life. Her daughter, Topsannah, succumbed to illness shortly after their capture. With the deaths of Peta Nocona and Topsannah, Cynthia Ann sported the traditional short hair, a Comanche ritual to show mourning, until the day she died.

[41] National Register Properties in Oklahoma: Canute Service Station. http://www.ocgi.okstate.edu/shpo/shpopic.asp?id=94001611. Accessed 22 February 2010, 23.30 CST.

[42] Until the mid-19th century, buffalo numbered in the millions, but that number was beginning to wane with the introduction of buffalo hunting and hide trading in the Plains. Some Native American tribes worked in tandem with the hide hunters, while others fought the killings. With the push for American settlement and industrialization of the West after the Civil War, however, the buffalo slaughter began in earnest. Within a ten year time frame (from 1875 to 1885), all free roaming buffalo in the Southern Plains had vanished. Cattleman Charles Goodnight, despite his own involvement in the slaughter, recognized the historical significance of this decline. He was able to stock his ranch at Palo Duro Canyon with bison, which halted the Southern Plains' buffalo from total extinction.

[43] Welcome to Dodge City Kansas. http://www.visitdodgecity.org/index.aspx?NID=66. Accessed 29 December 2009, 12.02 CST.

www.ingramcontent.com/pod-product-compliance
Lightning Source LLC
Chambersburg PA
CBHW060827050426
42453CB00008B/612